Praise for *99 to 1*

"*99 to 1* gives a fresh ⸺⸺⸺⸺⸺⸺⸺⸺ anure—it doesn't do any good unless you spread it around." Tip: Pay special atten**⸺** to Chuck's 'What can we do' ideas. Read, absorb, and help sprea⸺

—Jim ⸺⸺⸺⸺⸺ ial radio commentator and author of *Swim Against the Current*

"Most businesses want a level playing field, which means terminating subsidies to the largest corporations, eliminating their use of tax havens, getting their money out of politics, and implementing other initiatives that will help create a vibrant and sustainable economy. Collins's proposals would boost enterprises that are rooted in our communities, create jobs, and protect the environment. That's good business."

—**David Levine, Executive Director, American Sustainable Business Council**

"There is a wide and growing disparity in the access to wealth in this country and across the world. Chuck Collins makes a compelling case for how we can work together—all 100 percent of us—to increase economic opportunity for all Americans."

—**Benjamin Todd Jealous, President and CEO, NAACP**

"Chuck Collins has delivered a powerful book on how the richest 1 percent have benefited from the sacrifices of working families—and why it's time to give back."

—**Richard Trumka, President, AFL-CIO**

"Chuck Collins succinctly sums up the history of how we got to the 99-versus-1 divide and provides sound solutions to restore the American Dream. Not only can these solutions bridge the wealth gap, but they can also heal some of our nation's deepest wounds. It's the primer for the 99 percent movement to rebuild an economy that works for the 100 percent."

—**Van Jones, President, Rebuild the Dream, and author of *The Green Collar Economy***

"So if you're rich, you're important; if you're not, you're worthless? That's no basis for a democratic society. Inequality messes with your mind and with the planet. Read this book and help put it right."

—**Richard Wilkinson, coauthor of *The Spirit Level***

"In this compelling and important book, Chuck Collins deftly exposes how the massive heist of national wealth by the richest 1 percent is wreaking havoc with our lives and devastating our world. Collins has been an intrepid advocate for greater equality for years, and he grasps the potential of the Occupy Wall Street movement to reverse the 'inequality death spiral.' This is a passionate and powerful call to arms to save the planet from the clutches of the greedy few."

—Linda McQuaig, coauthor of *Billionaires' Ball*

"Chuck Collins not only gives us the hard cold facts about inequality in America but also shares with us his gift for optimism. While he warns us that the hour is late to halt the downward spiral of inequality and environmental destruction, the power to make positive change still lies within us, waiting for the spark of renewal. With this remarkable book, Chuck is doing all that he can to rekindle that spark so that together we can fight for real change."

—Les Leopold, author of *The Looting of America*

"Chuck Collins concisely summarizes the data on income and wealth inequality and in a calm, clear voice reveals why inequality is increasing and what we must do to reverse it. If you are to read one thing this year about inequality and its impact on America, you must read this book. It's all here and very well done at that."

—Barry Bluestone, Dean, School of Public Policy and Urban Affairs, Northeastern University

"This is the best popular economics book of 2012. Occupy your mind with Collins's barn burner. You'll understand why inequality has become America's biggest crisis and why the Occupy Movement has captured the imagination of millions around the world. This riveting tale of America as two cities will stay with you for years to come and—watch out! It may rouse you to action on the solutions that Collins spells out with perfect precision."

—Charles Derber, author of *Corporation Nation* and *Greed to Green*

99 TO 1

99 TO 1

HOW **WEALTH INEQUALITY** IS WRECKING THE WORLD AND WHAT WE CAN DO ABOUT IT

CHUCK COLLINS

A publication of the
New Economy Working Group

BK®

Berrett–Koehler Publishers, Inc.
San Francisco
a BK Currents book

Berrett-Koehler Publishers, Inc.
235 Montgomery Street, Suite 650
San Francisco, CA 94104-2916
Tel: (415) 288-0260   Fax: (415) 362-2512   www.bkconnection.com

Ordering Information
Quantity sales. Special discounts are available on quantity purchases by corporations, associations, and others. For details, contact the "Special Sales Department" at the Berrett-Koehler
address above.

Individual sales. Berrett-Koehler publications are available through most bookstores. They can
also be ordered directly from Berrett-Koehler: Tel: (800) 929-2929; Fax: (802) 864-7626; www.
bkconnection.com

Orders for college textbook/course adoption use. Please contact Berrett-Koehler: Tel: (800)
929-2929; Fax: (802) 864-7626.

Orders by U.S. trade bookstores and wholesalers. Please contact Ingram Publisher Services,
Tel: (800) 509-4887; Fax: (800) 838-1149; E-mail: customer.service@ingrampublisherservices.
com; or visit www.ingrampublisherservices.com/Ordering for details about electronic ordering.

Berrett-Koehler and the BK logo are registered trademarks of Berrett-Koehler Publishers, Inc.

Printed in the United States of America

Berrett-Koehler books are printed on long-lasting acid-free paper. When it is available, we choose
paper that has been manufactured by environmentally responsible processes. These may include
using trees grown in sustainable forests, incorporating recycled paper, minimizing chlorine in
bleaching, or recycling the energy produced at the paper mill.

Library of Congress Cataloging-in-Publication Data

Collins, Chuck, 1959–
    99 to 1 : how wealth inequality is wrecking the world and what we can do about it /
Chuck Collins.
        p. cm.
    Includes bibliographical references and index.
    ISBN 978-1-60994-592-3 (pbk.)
    1. Income distribution. 2. Poverty. 3. Wealth. 4. Equality. 5. Economic policy.
I. Title. II. Title: Ninety-nine to one.
    HC79.I5C632 2012
    339.2'2–dc23

                                                                                      2012001968

First Edition

17 16 15 14 13 12   10 9 8 7 6 5 4 3 2 1

BOOK PRODUCED BY: Westchester Book Group
COVER DESIGN: Morris Design
COVER ART: Moodboard / 123RF
INTERIOR ILLUSTRATION: Precision Graphics
COPYEDITOR: Sue Warga
INDEXER: Julie Grady

In celebration of Felice Yeskel, who planted the seeds but didn't live to see the fruit on the trees. May the light perpetual shine upon her.

For N., wonderful daughter, who will carry the torch for the next generation.

For M., muse, sage, and spark.

Contents

Foreword

BARBARA EHRENREICH

Several years ago, on the eve of the 2008 Great Recession, I had an argument with Chuck Collins about inequality. He had just launched a project called the Working Group on Extreme Inequality, with the goal of educating the public about the huge gaps in wealth and income that separate Americans—a goal that I heartily shared. But my cynical question was, who cares? As Brookings Institution economist Carol Graham had stated that year, "The only people who are bothered by inequality are rich liberals."

In my argument with Chuck, I cited "Joe the Plumber," who opposed Obama's proposal to raise taxes on those earning more than $250,000 a year because he firmly expected to pass that benchmark himself—once he had established his own plumbing business, that is. This is the great American delusion, I argued: that through hard work, cunning, positive thinking, or prayer, anyone can become a multimillionaire almost overnight. For most people, then, inequality is not a problem—just a goad to greater achievement.

Well, Chuck was right. In the years since our conversation, the grossly top-heavy American financial system crashed, revealing that inequality is a dangerously destabilizing force. The rich had invested heavily in a variety of shaky credit schemes, which the poor and the middle class were desperate—or deluded—enough to fall for. In the last few years, with the economy in a grinding recession, we learned just how costly extreme inequality is, as measured by unemployment, foreclosures, and rising poverty rates.

But Chuck Collins explains all this far better than I could—lucidly, compellingly, and, when necessary, graphically. As an activist who has worked with both ends of the economic spectrum—low-income people struggling to get by and millionaires concerned about the future of our country—he is one of our premier experts on inequality. And after you read this book, you'll be another one.

Preface

Extreme inequalities of wealth are undermining much of what we hold dear.

Our society is in the throes of an inequality death spiral as disparities of wealth and power compound and worsen. This polarization is wrenching communities apart, undermining democratic institutions, making us sick and unhappy, and destabilizing our economy.

For twenty years, I've been part of efforts to educate the wider public about the dangers of these extreme income and wealth inequalities. It has been a discouraging time. Frequently I've been told, "Inequality is not the right way to talk about the economy" and "Americans don't really care about inequality." Sometimes I wondered if these naysayers were right.

In the last year, however, the conversation about economic inequality has dramatically changed. The Occupy Wall Street movement contributed to a huge shift in the conversation with the "We are the 99 percent" movement. But other threads have also emerged from around the planet, such as street protests and rebellions across the Arab world and Europe.

This book brings together, in one place, a vivid picture of the state of U.S. and global inequality. More important, it offers paths forward in how we will reverse these inequalities.

The first part of the book answers two questions: Who are the 1 percent and the 99 percent? How do the 1 percent and Wall Street wield power? The middle chapters of this book examine how these inequalities emerged and why they matter. The final chapters examine the movements to build an economy for the 100 percent. They offer policy ideas and a vision to move us toward a new, healthy, and sustainable economy.

Some commentators have rejected the simplicity of the 99 to 1 framework, rightly pointing out that it glosses over the divisions and diversity within both segments. Obviously, 99 to 1 is part demographic and part symbolic. But it is a meaningful and powerful lens to understand this moment in history, as this book will explain.

Some are offended by the focus on the 1 percent and its implied framework of "class war." (We surveyed hundreds of people to enlist ideas for what to title this book. One funny suggestion was "Eating the Rich: Recipes for Ending the Class War.")

My own perspective is that we need everyone—the whole 100 percent—to be engaged in changing our imbalanced society. We need every potential ally we can find. I grew up in the 1 percent, so I don't hate them—they're my family and childhood friends. I know they are not monolithic. And I'm inspired by the large percentage of the 1 percent who believe the economy should work for everyone and are willing to work for change. In chapter 8, I discuss the important role of the 1 percent in working for an economy for the 100 percent.

Every couple of days I log on and read the profiles and pictures that people post at one of the "We are the 99 percent" websites. One thing I know for certain: the underlying conditions that gave rise to the 99 percent movement—joblessness, economic insecurity, bloated CEO pay, unpayable student loan obligations, grinding poverty, and collapsing middle-class livelihoods—are not going away soon.

At the same time, a segment of the top 1 percent and a few thousand transnational corporations have a tight grip on our media and political process and have been blocking change. They have been materially enriched from decades of extreme inequality.

The pressure will keep building until change occurs.

I am optimistic that we have a very good chance of not only reversing the worst of these inequalities but also organizing an economy for the 100 percent that responds to the global ecological and economic challenges that we face together.

Each of us has a role to play. We need all hands on deck. My intention for this book is to contribute to this movement.

CHUCK COLLINS

Boston, Massachusetts
February 2012

INTRODUCTION

We Are the 99 Percent

They will put up with poverty, servitude, and barbarism, but they will not endure aristocracy.
—Alexis de Tocqueville (1805–1859)

Photo © John Quigley.

In the fall of 2011, a website emerged urging people to share a photograph and story of their experience being in the 99 percent. One young woman wrote,

> I used to dream about becoming the first woman president. Now I dream about getting a job with health insurance.[1]

A twenty-seven-year-old veteran of the Iraq War described how he enlisted to protect the American people but discovered he "ended up making profits for politically connected contractors."

> I returned to a country whose economy had been devastated by bankers with the same connections and the same lack of ethics. . . . This is the second time I've fought for my country and the first time I've known my enemy. I am the 99 percent.[2]

One handwritten sign simply says:

> I am twenty. I can't afford college. There aren't many jobs I qualify for, and the rest "just aren't hiring." Tell me, what exactly am I living for? I am the 99 percent.

On another website, organized to give voice to members of the 1 percent who support the 99 percent, an investment advisor named Carl Schweser wrote,

> I made millions studying the math of mortgages and bonds and helping bankers pass the Chartered Financial Analyst Exam.
> It isn't fair that I have retired in comfort after a career working with financial instruments while people who worked as nurses, teachers, soldiers, and so on are worried about paying for their future, their health care, and their children's educations.
> They are the backbone of this country that allowed me to succeed.
> I am willing to pay more taxes so that everyone can look forward to a secure future like I do.
> I am the 1%.

> I stand with the 99%.
> (Which equals 100% of America.)
> Tax me.[3]

These are the stories that are propelling a new conversation in the United States and the world. And so are these statistics:

- The 1 percent has 35.6 percent of all private wealth, more than the bottom 95 percent combined. The 1 percent has 42.4 percent of all financial wealth, more than the bottom 97 percent combined.[4]
- The 400 wealthiest individuals on the Forbes 400 list have more wealth than the bottom 150 million Americans.[5]
- In 2010, 25 of the 100 largest U.S. companies paid their CEO more than they paid in U.S. taxes. This is largely because corporations in the global 1 percent use offshore tax havens to dodge their U.S. taxes.[6]
- In 2010, the 1 percent earned 21 percent of all income.[7]
- Between 1983 and 2009, over 40 percent of all wealth gains flowed to the 1 percent and 82 percent of wealth gains went to the top 5 percent. The bottom 60 percent lost wealth over this same period.
- The world's 1 percent, almost entirely millionaires and billionaires, owns $42.7 trillion, more than the bottom 3 billion residents of Earth.
- While the middle-class standard of living implodes, sales of luxury items such as $10,000 wristwatches and Lamborghini sports cars are skyrocketing.
- Between 2001 and 2010, the United States borrowed over $1 trillion to give wealthy taxpayers with incomes over $250,000 substantial tax breaks, including the 2001 Bush-era tax cuts.[8]

Most Americans have tolerated these growing inequalities for decades—in large part because they believed that everyone had a chance to climb the ladder to success. The economic crisis of 2008 and the eloquent cries of the "We are the 99 percent" movement have shattered this illusion of an opportunity society.

Seven Messages of This Book

More and more people are paying attention to the extreme inequalities of wealth that have emerged in our midst, and they are asking: How did it get this way? How did rules get changed? Who is this 1 percent? Are they all bad? Why do so many laws passed by Congress benefit the 1 percent instead of the 99 percent? And, most important: Can we reverse it? Is there hope for the 99 percent?

You don't have to read the whole book to get a quick response. I have seven intentions for this book, points that I hope you as reader will take away.

Inequality Matters to You. Think about what you care deeply about: kids, health, education, the environment, culture, housing, and the amount of free time you have. In every area that you care about, the extreme wealth inequalities of the last several decades have damaged and undermined these conditions.

We Are Living in an Inequality Death Spiral. These growing inequalities of wealth, power, and opportunity interact in a frighteningly dynamic way to contribute to a downward spiral of worsening social, ecological, and economic conditions. Compounding inequalities are like a black hole, sucking the life energy out of our communities, and destroying our health, livelihoods, well-being, and happiness. We really have no choice but to throw our energies into stopping these forces.

99 to 1 Is a Powerful Lens for Understanding This Historical Moment. The 99 to 1 framework is a powerful way to understand what is happening in our society and economy. It is a way for people to situate their experience and understand the dramatic shifts that have occurred in our lifetimes. It also has significant political implications for elections. Some candidates will run as "advocates for the 99 percent" and challenge their opponents as "serving only the 1 percent." We should embrace the 99 to 1 framework and work with it.

Some People Are Responsible for Excessive Inequality. A simple explanation of how inequality has grown is that a small segment of the top 1 percent—with an organized base in Wall Street's financial institutions—has worked over many decades to rig the rules of the economy to favor the 1 percent at the expense of the 99 percent. The rules have been tilted in favor of those who own large amounts of assets at the expense of wage earners. These rules include government actions and policies related to taxation, global trade, regulation, and public spending. These rule changes have led to massive imbalances of wealth and power that jeopardize peace and prosperity across the globe.

The 1 Percent Is Not Monolithic. Not everyone in the top 1 percent is to blame for rigging the rules. Nor is everyone in the bottom 99 percent without responsibility for the growth of inequality. Within the 1 percent are people who have devoted their lives to building a healthy economy that works for everyone. The focus of our concern and organizing should be the "rule riggers" within the 1 percent— those who use their power and wealth to influence the game so that they and their corporations get more power and wealth. This is good news, because the rule riggers, though powerful, don't hold all the cards. And there are huge numbers of allies in the 1 percent who are part of the movements for a more fair and equitable world.

Corporations and Business Are Not Monolithic. Just as individuals in the 1 percent are diverse actors, the 1 percent of corporations are also not unified. There are several thousand transnational corporations—the Wall Street inequality machine—that are the drivers of rule changes. But they are the minority. There are millions of other built-to-last corporations and Main Street businesses that strengthen our communities and have a stake in an economy that works for the 100 percent. We must defend ourselves from the bad actors—the built-to-loot companies whose business model is focused on shifting costs onto society, shedding jobs, and extracting wealth from our communities and the healthy economy.

These Inequalities Are Reversible. Here's the good news: we can reverse the inequality death spiral. We can change the conditions that are worsening inequality. Indeed, we did this once before, in the last century after the first Gilded Age. The seeds of a new social movement to reverse these wealth inequalities are sprouting across the planet.

This book is the story of what has happened and how we can build an economy that works for everyone.

1 Coming Apart at the Middle

An imbalance between rich and poor is the oldest and most fatal ailment of all republics.
—Plutarch (c. 46–120 CE)

For more than three decades, the United States has undertaken a dangerous social experiment: How much inequality can a democratic self-governing society handle? How far can we stretch the gap between the super-rich 1 percent and everyone else before something snaps?

We have pulled apart. Over a relatively short period of time, since the election of Ronald Reagan in 1980, a massive share of global income and wealth has funneled upward into the bank accounts of the richest 1 percent—and, within that group, the richest one-tenth of 1 percent.

This has been not just a U.S. trend but a global tendency, as the wealthiest 1 percent of the planet's citizens delinked from the rest of humanity in terms of wealth, opportunity, life expectancy, and quality of life.

The New Grand Canyon: Extreme Inequality

There has always been economic inequality in the world and within the United States, even during what is called the "shared prosperity" decades after World War II, 1947 to 1977. But since the late 1970s, we've entered into a period of extreme inequality, a dizzying reordering of society.

This radical upward redistribution of wealth was not a weather event but a human-created disaster. Segments of the organized 1 percent lobbied politicians and pressed for changes in the rules in the political area, rules governing such areas as trade, taxes, workers, and corporations. *In a nutshell: (1) the rules of the economy have been changed to benefit asset owners at the expense of wage earners, and (2) these rule changes have benefited global corporations at the expense of local businesses.* There has been a triumph of capital and a betrayal of work.

The story of the last three decades is that working hard and earning wages didn't move you ahead. "Real income"—excluding inflation—has remained stagnant or fallen since the late 1970s. Meanwhile, income from wealth (such as investments, property, and stocks) has taken off on a rocket launcher. Today, the dirty secret about how to get very wealthy in this economy is to start with wealth.

Most Americans are aware, on some level, that the rich have gotten steadily richer. We've seen the reports about mansions being torn down to build new mega-mansions. Or the CEOs who are paid more in one day than their average employees earn in a year. We've watched the middle-class dream collapse for ourselves or loved ones around us. We've intuitively sensed a shift in the culture toward individualism and the celebration of excessive wealth while also witnessing an erosion of the community institutions that we all depend on, such as schools, libraries, public transportation, and parks.

The Inequality Chat Room

Meanwhile, the public conversation over inequality has slowly progressed since 1980. In the late 1980s, the main debate was over whether inequality existed at all. Pundits and scholars squabbled over the data. Kevin Phillips, a former speechwriter for President Richard Nixon, wrote a book called *The Politics of Rich and Poor* that decried the first stage of income inequality in the 1980s.[1] Others countered that his facts were wrong or disputed his methodology.[2]

By 2000, however, there was a strong consensus about the facts of income inequality. Speeches by conservatives Alan Greenspan and President George W. Bush decried the troubling trends in income disparity.[3]

The public disagreement shifted to a dispute over what caused these inequalities and whether they mattered at all. Most agreed that poverty—inadequate income, lack of resources, and social exclusion—is a problem. But does it matter how wealthy the wealthy are? Does the concentration of wealth matter to the larger society?

This is where the debate has remained stalled for many years. Some analysts argue that inequality doesn't matter as long as there is mobility, opportunity, and poverty alleviation. And some believe inequality is good because it motivates people at the bottom of the economic ladder to work harder.

Most of us have been too busy to monitor the changing trends in the economy. Some of us have been on a financial treadmill, working harder and running faster to stay in the same place. Or we've lost ground, watching our dreams of future economic stability slip away. The real inequality story has crept up on most of us while we weren't looking.

A Tolerance for Inequality

Now we're waking up. Attitude polls indicate that people are much more alarmed about wealth inequality and the destruction it has wreaked upon our economic lives.

The United States has historically had a very high tolerance for inequality compared to the rest of the world. For decades, the majority attitude toward stories of excessive wealth was "So what?"[4]

Prior to 2008, polls reflected that a majority of Americans, while troubled by growing inequality, believed that income inequality was a result of varying degrees of individual merit. In other words, people's economic status was a reflection of deservedness—hard work, intelligence, and effort. Most people were not troubled by the fact that a small sliver of people was becoming fantastically wealthy—as long as that wealth was fairly attained and that others had the same opportunity in terms of social mobility.

But since 2008, public attitudes have shifted. The middle-class standard of living has imploded, with once stable families now experiencing economic insecurity. And intergenerational mobility in the United States—the promise that the circumstances of one's children will likely be better than one's own—is now lower than in other industrialized countries. A greater percentage of the public now believes that the lopsided distribution of wealth is a problem. More people view great fortunes as the result of the wealthy 1 percent rigging the rules of the game in their favor.[5]

Even with growing unease over inequality, the issue has remained sequestered from public debate. The policy debates in Washington, D.C., appear disconnected from the real concerns of ordinary Americans. For example, the U.S. Congress appears preoccupied with matters such as the national debt and debt ceiling, rather than deep unemployment, home foreclosures, corporate tax dodging, and the collapse of the middle class.

Most of us have felt powerless to change these growing inequality dynamics and the reckless and shortsighted actions of the powerful. This is, in part, because most of the corporate media that dominates our airwaves didn't think inequality was a topic worthy of much public scrutiny or discussion.

Until recently. Thanks to protesters occupying Wall Street and the "99 percent" movement across the world, the conversation began to shift. And even as protests morph into new forms, a fundamental change in attitudes is under way.

Media analysis during the summer and fall of 2011 found that media attention shifted away from a focus on debt to a focus on unemployment, inequality, and Wall Street.[6] By October 2011, two-thirds of the public believed wealth should be more evenly distributed and that Congress should reverse tax cuts for corporations and increase income taxes on millionaires.[7]

These feelings about inequality are unlikely to change in coming years. People's deep anger has been given credence. The eloquent personal statements appearing at places such as the We Are the 99 Percent website give expression to the suffering, pain, insecurity, and anger that have been invisible for far too long. There is no going back.

The simple demand that *we should have an economy that works for everyone, not just the richest 1 percent*, is powerful, resonant, and inspiring.

The current political system, dominated by the concerns of the top 1 percent and captured by a small segment of global corporations, is incapable of responding to demands for greater shared prosperity. And so the pressure will continue to build for real change.

The 99 Percent Movement

At the Occupy Wall Street protests, an early hand-lettered protest sign stated, WE ARE THE 99 PERCENT. Soon a website emerged, with individuals writing their "we are the 99 percent" stories.[8]

One military veteran wrote that she had friends die for this country and is grateful not to have student loans. But her fiancé will have over $75,000 in loans.

> I am a licensed practical nurse with no job prospects. I haven't been employed in over a year. . . . I couldn't get a job as a waitress as I was overqualified. I am the 99%.[9]

Another young woman writes that she is unable to save for her February wedding because she's working in a restaurant busing tables for $8 an hour to help her father pay off $23,000 in student loans and medical bills.

> I want to start a family someday, but the future looks dim.
>   I'm not even 20 years old yet and I already feel like debt will consume my whole life. I am the 99%.

"We are the 99 percent" has become the rallying cry for a new way of looking at the economy. Through the lens of 99 versus 1, we can ask questions such as: Will this policy help the bottom 99 percent? Is this politician a servant of the 1 percent? Which side are you on?

The First Gilded Age: 1890–1929

The history of inequality in the last hundred years reveals that our nation previously lived through a period of extreme inequality and reversed those trends, thanks in part to people coming together to press for change. Understanding this history will help us roll back the current chapter of inequality we are living through.

The last time U.S. society experienced such extreme levels of inequality was during the long Gilded Age from 1890 to 1928. In the aftermath of the industrial revolution, wealth inequalities became glaring and stark.

The great robber baron fortunes, those of Rockefeller, Carnegie, and Vanderbilt, exercised tremendous economic, political, and cultural power. And a handful of giant corporations—what a century ago were called "concentrations" and "trusts"—dominated the political system with their short-term interests.

Scholars estimate that around 1929, the wealthiest 1 percent owned as much as 44 percent of all private wealth, compared to about 36.5 percent today.[10] Equally alarming was the rate of corporate consolidation and the formation of monopolies, especially in railroads, banking, and heavy industry such as steel production. Between 1897 and 1904, some 4,227 firms consolidated into 257 companies.[11]

Historian James Huston observed that "in a wave of pools, trusts, and then mergers, large business enterprise took over the core production of the American economy. The change induced a panic mentality among commentators who feared that now the distribution of wealth was becoming permanently warped and unsuitable for republican institutions."[12]

During this first Gilded Age there was a robust debate about the consequences of inequality. Social commentators, religious leaders, and industrialists such as Andrew Carnegie rang the alarm about the threat that concentrated wealth and power posed to our democracy, economy, and culture. They believed it shattered all the ideals upon which the U.S. experiment in self-governance was founded.[13]

Journalist Henry Demarest Lloyd characterized the era as "wealth against commonwealth," with the corrosive power of concentrated wealth undermining the larger common good. After the American Revolution, which eliminated the hereditary rule of monarchy, the United States was now dangerously close to becoming a plutocracy—a society ruled by its wealthy elite. Exposés of the period documented the almost complete capture of the U.S. Senate by wealthy and corporate interests.[14] At the time, a young Louis Brandeis stated, "We can have concentrated wealth in the hands of a few or we can have democracy. But we cannot have both."[15]

Being in the bottom 99 percent in 1910 undoubtedly was bleak. It must have seemed at the time that the concentrations of wealth and power were unchangeable. It would have been almost impossible to envision back then that the next generation would live in a flowering period of relative equality and shared prosperity.

The extended Gilded Age ended in 1929, in part because of the Great Depression and two world wars. But a significant factor was that popular movements and political leaders rebelled against the corrosive impact of extreme inequality. Religious leaders, urban workers, rural populists and farmers, and civic-oriented politicians were champions of fundamental rule changes and reforms.[16]

These reformers pressed for policies to reduce concentrated wealth and broaden prosperity. They advocated for rule changes such as passage of the federal income tax and estate tax in 1916 with the explicit goal of reducing income and wealth concentrations. [17] Other rule changes included legislation banning child labor, breaking up corporate monopolies (trust busting), expanding corporate regulation, and instituting social expenditures to address poverty and poor housing conditions.

These changes had the positive impact of greatly reducing wealth disparities. The share of wealth owned by the 1 percent dropped from 44 percent in 1929 to 20 percent in 1970.[18]

Growing Together: The Years of Shared Prosperity, 1947–1977

The shared prosperity in the years after World War II was the result of rule changes made between 1930 and the 1960s that focused on expansion of the middle class, not on enriching the 1 percent. Some economists called this period of relative equality the "great compression" because of the ways that U.S. society equalized out.[19]

Policy Changes That Reversed the First Gilded Age

Why did this happen? Part of the reason was the collapse of fortunes during the Great Depression. But, equally important, our society advanced a two-part pro-equality agenda that reduced wealth concentrations and promoted expansion of the middle class.

Pro-Middle-Class Agenda. The rules of the economy were organized to promote the expansion of a middle class, particularly among white households. Tax revenue was invested in expanding educational opportunity, homeownership, and infrastructure.

- *Expansion of free higher education.* Programs such as the GI Bill provided debt-free college educations to more than 11 million returning veterans between 1945 and 1955. Benefits went beyond military veterans to include additional groups via Pell Grants, other educational grants, and low-interest loans.
- *Homeownership expansion.* Government programs aimed at boosting homeownership, such as the Farmers Home Administration, Federal Housing Administration mortgage insurance, and housing loans provided through the Veterans Administration, provided low fixed-rate mortgages for terms as long as forty years. Between 1945 and 1968 the percentage of the U.S. population that became homeowners expanded from 44 percent to 63 percent. This investment put a generation of homeowners on the road to wealth building.[20]

Reducing the concentration of wealth. Emerging out of the Great Depression, a number of policies were boldly aimed at reducing the concentration of wealth and corporate power.

- *Taxing high incomes and wealth.* In 1916, Congress instituted both progressive inheritance taxes and high income taxes. Over a generation, this greatly reduced wealth disparities and also raised revenue to pay for the middle-class agenda.
- *Oversight and taxing of corporations.* Corporations were brought under considerably more public oversight after the Depression and were required to contribute tax revenue to the war effort and the building of society's infrastructure.
- *Boosting labor power in relation to Wall Street power.* Rules were changed to permit greater worker organization, which gave workers a greater voice in the economy.

These rule changes resulted in widely shared prosperity across all segments of U.S. society. In the thirty years after World War II, from 1947 to 1977, real income growth was seen across the economic

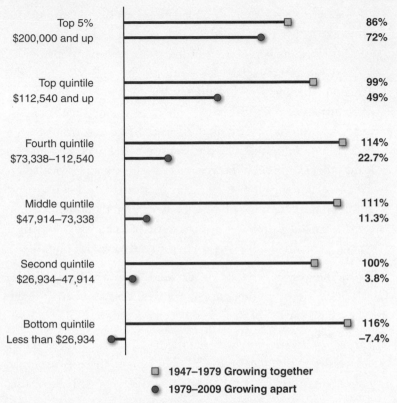

| | 1947–1979 Growing together |
| | 1979–2009 Growing apart |

Figure 1. Growing together after World War II and pulling apart after 1979.

spectrum. The highest-income 1 percent saw their incomes rise during this period at the same rate as the rest of the society. The rising tide lifted almost all boats across the society, particularly for whites and men.

There's an important historical lesson and political point here. We have reversed extreme inequality that existed once before in U.S. history. Because these inequalities are human-made, they are not impermeable to change.

Pulling Apart: 1977 to Present

The "growing together" years after World War II were a stark contrast to the "pulling apart" period of unequal growth of income and wealth over the last thirty-five years. In coming chapters, we will explore the reasons extreme inequality has grown. But part of the story is simple: the rules governing the economy were tilted to benefit the wealthiest 1 percent at the expense of the 99 percent, and to benefit the top Wall Street corporations at the expense of Main Street businesses.

Starting in the late 1970s, as many large U.S. corporations established global assembly lines, real wages for much of the U.S. population began to stagnate. For the bottom 20 percent, real wages actually declined between 1976 and 1990.

These dismal wage trends would have been worse if not for two factors that masked their real impact. The first was the increasing number of hours worked per household, especially with more women entering the paid labor force. This meant that some households could maintain their standard of living in the face of rising health care and housing costs, even as real wages declined.[21]

The second factor was easy access to credit. Households in the bottom 80 percent borrowed heavily to fill in for declining or stagnant wages. They utilized credit cards and high-interest consumer loans, paying interest rates over 20 percent in some cases. If they owned a home, they often borrowed against the equity in their property.[22]

For millions of households, wage stagnation and falling wealth resulted in greater poverty and job insecurity. For others, debt and overwork fueled a vast illusion of middle-class affluence, as consumption expanded even as wages fell. People bought new cars and flat-screen TVs and went to Red Lobster for dinner. But this middle-class consumption was based on working more hours and borrowing, not on real wage growth. As we shall see, this sowed the seeds for the economic meltdown of 2008.

2 Who Is the 1 Percent?

We can have concentrated wealth in the hands of a few or we can have democracy. But we cannot have both.
—Louis Brandeis (1856–1941)

The "1 percent" framework is a useful lens for understanding the dramatic changes that have occurred in the last several decades. It is a real demographic we can pinpoint and picture as well as a symbolic reference to those primarily responsible for the polarization of wealth in our Union.

The "1 percent" icon has obvious limitations, too. It suggests we should focus on wealthy individuals when we also should be thinking about the role of the wealthiest corporations, sometimes summarized as "Wall Street." In chapter 5, we will discuss the Wall Street inequality machine and the interaction between the individual 1 percent and corporations.

The other limitation with the concept "99 to 1" is it presumes that everyone in the 1 percent thinks and acts the same. Within the 1 percent are some people who have dedicated their lives to building a better world for the 100 percent. The focus of our wrath should be on the segment of the 1 percent—the game riggers and rule fixers—who use their wealth and power selfishly to perpetuate their own privilege, wealth, and power.

The 1 percent is not a static group. For example, someone could be in the top 1 percent of income earners but not the top 1 percent of wealth holders. There are people at the bottom end of the richest 1 percent—mere millionaires—who will point out how their circumstances are radically different from those of a billionaire listed on the Forbes 400. This is true. Someone with $5 million in net worth has considerably less economic and political power than the billionaires George Soros and David Koch.

The benefits and privileges that flow to the 1 percent are, of course, not limited to just the 1 percent. There are people in the top 2 percent and even the top 20 percent who saw their wealth expand dramatically by virtue of the rule changes benefiting the super-rich.

The data demonstrate that the closer one is to the top of the economic pyramid, the larger one's share of wealth and income. This is because income from investments, largely held by those in the top 1 percent, has been higher, whereas income from work and wages has stayed flat.

The 1 Percent Club

So what does it take to join the 1 percent? How much wealth and income do they have? And what about the richest one-tenth of 1 percent? How can we distinguish between the active rule fixers and the passive part of the 1 percent?

The U.S. population in 2010 was over 315 million people in 152 million households. So 1 percent of the population was roughly 3 million people in 1.5 million households.

There are a number of measures of what constitutes the 1 percent, including examining both annual income and wealth (the latter, also called net worth, being defined as what you own minus what you owe). These two groups—the top 1 percent of income and the top 1 percent of wealth—largely overlap, but not entirely. There are many with high incomes but low net worth. And there are many with vast wealth but relatively low incomes—at least according to their tax returns.

Income

To join the top 1 percent of income earners, you must make over $500,000 per year. That's the entrance level for the club. The average income of the 1 percent is $1.5 million.[1]

In 2010, the top 1 percent in annual earnings made over 21 percent of the national income. The percentage of income flowing to the top 1 percent has steadily risen over recent decades. In 1979, the top 1 percent earned 8 percent of the national income. By 2007, their share had increased to over 23 percent.[2]

Between 1979 and 2007, the top 1 percent took in almost 60 percent of all income gains. The inflation-adjusted average incomes of the 1 percent grew 224 percent during these years. The bottom 90 percent received only 8.6 percent of income gains and saw their incomes rise just 5 percent.[3]

Figure 2. The 1 percent share of total pre-tax income, 1913–2009.

Income tells one piece of the story, the amount of money flowing into someone's bank account in a given year. But wealth—including savings, investments, and property ownership—tells us about enduring power, stability, and security.

Wealth

Wealth is everything you own, minus what you owe. So private wealth includes houses, land, stocks, bonds, speedboats, and diamond rings—material wealth that can be bought and sold.

To join the top 1 percent of wealth holders, you must have a net worth (assets minus liabilities) over $5 million. The average wealth of someone in the top 1 percent is $14.1 million, according to an analysis of Federal Reserve data conducted by the Economic Policy Institute.[4]

In 2009, the wealthiest 1 percent of households owned 35.6 percent of all private wealth. This is up from an estimated 20 percent in 1976.

Financial Assets. Most wealth statistics include ownership of homes, which for most households is their single biggest asset. To get a more accurate picture of the maldistribution of wealth, it is

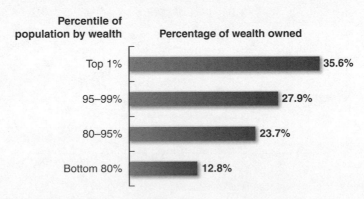

Figure 3. Distribution of U.S. wealth, 2009.

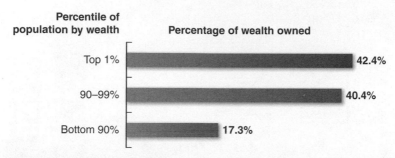

Figure 4. Distribution of U.S. stock market wealth, 2007.

useful to look at financial wealth—the ownership of financial assets such as stocks, bonds, currency, and savings.

The richest 1 percent owns 42.4 percent of all financial assets in 2009. The top 10 percent owns 82.8 percent of all financial assets, compared to 17.3 percent owned by the bottom 90 percent.[5]

Losing Wealth. Wealth inequality patterns were altered by the 2008 economic meltdown. But while the wealthy have largely recovered from their wealth declines, the majority of U.S. households have lost ground, probably permanently.

Research by the Economic Policy Institute examined the loss of wealth by those in the bottom 95 percent as home values plummeted.[6] Middle-class and African American households saw the biggest wealth losses.

In summary, between 1983 and 2009, 82 percent of all wealth gains flowed to the richest 5 percent. The bottom 60 percent did not share in the wealth expansion of this period, having less wealth in 2009 than in 1983.

Inside the 1 Percent

It may seem amusing to consider diversity among millionaires and billionaires, but there is a stunning divergence within the top 1 percent.

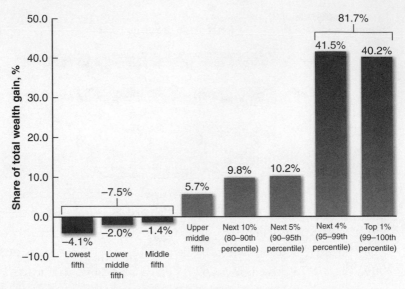

Figure 5. Most wealth gains go to top 5 percent: share of total wealth gain, 1983–2009.
Source: Mishel analysis of Wolff in Allegretto (2010).

This stratification reveals something about power and status in the United States and about who has the most power to shift the economy to work for the 100 percent. It also might help us pinpoint the game fixers within the 1 percent.

A Tour of Richistan

Robert Frank, whose full-time beat as a journalist is to chronicle the super-wealthy for the *Wall Street Journal*, offered a helpful construct in his book *Richistan: A Journey Through the American Wealth Boom and the Lives of the New Rich.*[7] He makes a distinction between what he calls Lower Richistan, Middle Richistan, Upper Richistan, and Billionaireville. Frank views wealth as a more important indicator than annual income in explaining status and power differences. What follows is a combination of Frank's framework and my analysis.

Lower Richistan is home to the approximately 8 million households with wealth between $1 million and $10 million. They are in the top 3 percent. This group inhabits the affluent suburbs surrounding most metropolitan areas, home to those who patronize country clubs, gourmet restaurants, and luxury resorts. But there are also millionaire-next-door households, thrifty folks who don't lead ostentatious lives and whose wealth grew steadily after World War II.[8] Their wealth comes from salaries, ownership of small businesses, and stock investments. The value of their primary home is over $1 million. They still fly on commercial airlines, but sometimes sit in first class.

Middle Richistan is home to the 2 million households with wealth between $10 million and $100 million. They are securely in the 1 percent. Their wealth comes from business ownership, investments, and some earned income. The value of their primary home is around $4 million, but they have multiple homes. At the upper end, they are flying private jets.

Upper Richistan is where you find the roughly 10,000 households with wealth over $100 million. Their ranks include entrepreneurs, hedge fund managers, and CEOs, along with heirs to multigenerational wealth dynasties. The value of their primary residence averages about $16 million. They fly private jets. Family offices help them administer their money and philanthropic activities, and trained house staff and other employees manage their various properties and residences. Frank writes, "When you live in Upper Richistan, your entire philosophy of money changes. You realize that you can't possibly spend all of your fortune, or even part of it, in your lifetime and that your money will probably grow over the years even if you spend lavishly. So Upper Richistanis plan their finances for the next hundred years. They don't buy mutual funds; they buy timber land, oil rigs and office towers."[9]

Billionaireville is the enclave for an estimated 700 to 1,000 households, some of which have managed to keep themselves off the Forbes 400 list (such as Steve Forbes himself) and hide their wealth in various offshore redoubts. They move from house to house—actually, more like compound to compound—with servants flying ahead to prepare for dinner parties and seasonal activities.

At the Top of the 1 Percent

The data show that in the last three decades, the richer you are, the larger the percentage of income and wealth that has flowed in your direction. The richest one-tenth of the 1 percent (or, put another way, the top 1 out of the top 1,000 households) have seen even more dramatic gains in income and wealth than the mere millionaires. These are households with incomes starting at $7.5 million.[10]

While the 1 percent realized 60 percent of all income gains between 1979 and 2007, the top one-tenth of 1 percent realized 36 percent of the total. The 1 percent saw their incomes go up 224 percent over these years, while the richest one-tenth of 1 percent saw theirs rise by 360 percent.[11]

And within that group the Forbes 400 are the biggest winners. They are easy to examine because they are profiled each year by *Forbes* magazine, providing ample research about who they are and their habits.

In 2011, the Forbes 400 held a combined $1.53 trillion in personal wealth, 12 percent higher than 2010. This was almost as high as 2007, on the eve of the economic meltdown, when they owned a combined $1.57 trillion.[12]

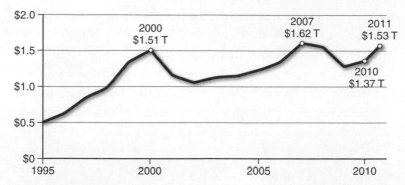

Figure 6. Top heavy: the total wealth of the Forbes 400 richest Americans, 1995–2010 (in trillions of 2010 dollars).

The threshold to join the Forbes 400 keeps rising. In 1982, when the magazine *Forbes* first ran the list, you needed at least $75 million to be included. There were only thirteen billionaires on the list, and the average wealth was $230 million. In 2011, the entrance level to the club was $1.05 billion; everyone profiled is a billionaire. The average wealth of a listee was $3.8 billion.

Even factoring in inflation, the expansion of wealth among this group is dizzying. When adjusted for inflation, the $230 million average in 1982 was equivalent to $540 million in 2010, not enough to join the present-day list. Between 1982 and 2011, the total combined fortunes of the Forbes 400, adjusted for inflation, mushroomed 612 percent.[13]

Among the 2011 Forbes 400, 122 inherited their way onto the list. Only forty-two are women. Forty-nine made their money through high-tech industries, while the largest number come from finance and real estate, two sectors that have rocked the domestic economy.[14]

The more income and wealth one has, the more the rules of the economy have been tilted in one's favor since the 1970s. For example, the richest four hundred taxpayers, according to the most recent IRS data, paid an effective tax rate of only 18.1 percent of their income, dramatically down from 43.1 percent in 1961.[15]

Within the 1 percent, there is a super-wealthy and powerful stratum whose power is interlocked with individuals and businesses connected to Wall Street and large corporations. In the next chapter, we will examine how the 1 percent uses its power.

The Global 1 Percent

A global vantage point is also helpful. Everyone in the top 1 percent in the United States is part of a tiny national and global echelon of high-income and wealth-holding individuals who have hugely benefited from the changing rules of the economy.

But even those in the 99 percent in the United States are probably in the top 5 percent globally. So we have a responsibility to look at the ways in which we cooperate with global rule changes that have worsened inequality. Only a small slice of the planetary 5 percent actively rigs the rules in a way that fuels wealth inequality. But we are all responsible for our inaction, because we tolerate the global pulling apart and accept the economic privileges of an international economy that benefits us at the expense of billions of others.

The drift toward extreme inequality is not limited to the United States. Across the world, the wealthiest 1 percent in every country has pulled apart from the 99 percent of their domestic economies. With the dynamics of capital income growing and wages remaining stagnant, the world's 1 percent have seen their global share of wealth explode.

In 2006, scholars from the United Nations University's World Institute for Development Economics Research published the first paper to tally, for the entire world, all the major elements of household wealth, everything from financial assets and debts to land, homes, and other tangible property.

This research, based on year 2000 data, found that the richest 1 percent of the world's adult population, individuals worth at least $514,512, owned 39.9 percent of the world's household wealth. This is greater than the wealth of the world's poorest 95 percent, those adults worth under $150,145, who together hold just 29.4 percent of the world's wealth.

Global wealth researchers found that the world's high-net-worth individuals surpassed their wealth levels prior to the 2007–2008 economic crisis. There are almost 11 million global millionaires, and their financial wealth now totals $42.7 trillion.[16]

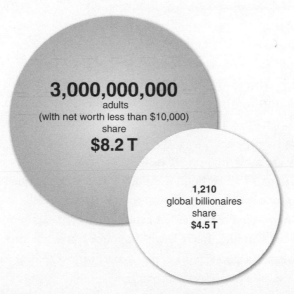

3,000,000,000
adults
(with net worth less than $10,000)
share
$8.2 T

1,210
global billionaires
share
$4.5 T

Figure 7. Global top heavy: 1,214 global billionaires have over half as much wealth as the bottom 3 billion occupants of the planet, 2010 (in trillions of dollars).

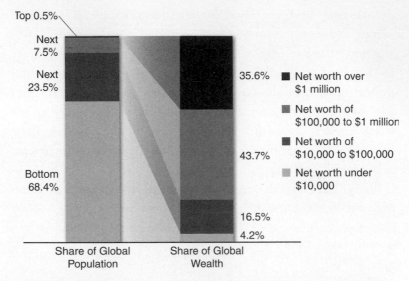

Top 0.5%

Next
7.5%

Next
23.5%

Bottom
68.4%

35.6%   ■ Net worth over
             $1 million

         ■ Net worth of
             $100,000 to $1 million

43.7%   ■ Net worth of
             $10,000 to $100,000

         ■ Net worth under
             $10,000

16.5%

4.2%

Share of Global   Share of Global
   Population   Wealth

Figure 8. Global population and wealth shares for adults at various levels of net worth, 2010.

At the pinnacle of global wealth are the planet's ultra-rich and billionaires. According to a new wealth research report by Wealth-X, there are 185,795 individuals worldwide who have at least $30 million in net worth. Together they hold a combined $25 trillion in wealth. A third of these individuals are in North America.[17]

There are more than 1,235 billionaires globally, with a combined net worth of $4.18 trillion. Their combined wealth equals over half the total wealth of the 3.01 billion adults around the world who, according to Credit Suisse, hold under $10,000 each in net worth. At the base of the global wealth pyramid are 1.1 billion people who own less than $1,000 each. According to Credit Suisse, 2.5 billion people are as yet "unbanked," possessing no measurable savings.[18]

Today, the super-wealthy in Mexico and India have more in common with their wealthy cohorts in Paris and New York City than they do with their own countrymen and -women in the bottom 99 percent of their native lands.

The 1 percent are global consumers, staying in fancy hotels, driving high-end cars, and purchasing luxury foods and beverages. They are traveling the world—and so is their wealth. Many move their money to offshore secrecy jurisdictions to avoid taxation in their native countries.

Elites in the global South—Africa, Asia, and Latin America—use the same offshore tax shelter systems as First World elites: Swiss bank accounts, shell corporations in the Isle of Man, and Caribbean tax havens such as the Cayman Islands.

3 How the 1 Percent Rigs the Rules of the Economy

A State divided into a small number of rich and a large number of poor will always develop a government manipulated by the rich to protect the amenities represented by their property.
—Harold Laski (1893–1950)

How does the 1 percent use its power?

Within the 1 percent, there are people who use their economic and political power differently. In one respect, the 1 percent is not much different from the population at large in that only a small segment is engaged in politics and actively advocating on policy matters. Some in the 1 percent care about the 100 percent and work for a fair and sustainable economy. Others are rule fixers, focused on rigging government policies in their favor to get more wealth and power. But the majority are unengaged and happy to watch their wealth accumulate without weighing in one way or another.

The game fixers maintain a worldview that justifies using every tool at their disposal to perpetuate and expand their wealth. Most believe they are the engines of the economic train, creating enterprises and wealth that pull everyone else along. This worldview is well captured in the introduction to the 2010 Forbes 400 survey.

Who cares whether somebody is worth $2 billion or $6 billion? We do. That personal stash is a critical barometer of how well the nation—and, to a degree, the world—is doing. By creating wealth, the people on our list help share epic financial trends, as well as shifts in leadership and policy, often providing the spark for innovation and entrepreneurship.[1]

They conflate extreme wealth with virtuous actions that are beneficial to the society as a whole. They believe government should step aside and not interfere with their actions—or, better yet, steer subsidies and tilt the rules in their favor. Some genuinely believe this serves the greater good. Others don't think much about the bottom 99 percent and through their inaction perpetuate the unequal status quo.

Unfortunately, three decades of rule changes in favor of the 1 percent, as we shall discuss, have almost destroyed the economy and ecology of the planet and shattered the lives of billions around the world. The system is now wired so that, from an economic and ecological point of view, the 1 percent are acting against their long-term self-interest.

Five Ways the 1 Percent Uses Its Power

The most powerful segment of the game riggers are the organized wealthy, people who use a wide variety of tools—political contributions, charitable giving, media ownership, and control over think tanks and advocacy groups—to tip the scales in their favor. There are five primary ways that the top 1 percent of wealthy individuals use their power and influence.

Political Influence

Policy makers pay attention to the 1 percent because of their wealth, influence, and campaign contributions. Not everyone who makes a political contribution is a game rigger. But the hyper-engaged among the 1 percent will channel millions directly to candidates, legislative issues, political parties, and a myriad of influence channels such as political action committees (PACs) and 501(c)(4) corporations.

Political scientist Larry Bartels has studied how lawmakers give preferential treatment to richer constituents.[2] There are several ways the top 1 percent directly influence politics.

Campaign Contributions. Only a tiny sliver of households give contributions of $200 or more to major-party candidates for federal office. In 2010, about one-third of 1 percent of the adult population gave $200, accounting for roughly two-thirds of all campaign contributions. The big donors in the 1 percent who max out their contributions by giving more than $2,400 are about 0.05 percent of the population. That's only 146,715 people out of a population of over 315 million.[3] This is why politicians listen so carefully to the organized 1 percent.

Personal Relationships with Elected Officials. Most members of Congress have personal relationships with game riggers in the 1 percent, even if the donors live outside their districts. They have been at fund-raisers together, broken bread together, and talked on the phone. According to research, the 1 percent is far more likely to have contacted their member of Congress than the average person. A study examining the super-rich in the Chicago area found that half the households with a median net worth of at least $7.5 million contacted their member of Congress and other high-level government officials.[4]

Higher Voter Turnout Among the 1 Percent. Probably least important in terms of political influence is the fact that the 1 percent vote in most elections. While 64 percent of registered voters cast a vote in 2008 election, almost 100 percent of 1 percent members voted.[5]

Charity Sector Influence

The majority of people in the 1 percent give to charity to make the world a better place. The game riggers use donations to charitable tax-exempt organizations to advance their economic interests. For example, some direct funds through private tax-exempt charitable foundations they control to fund research and policy advocacy organizations to actively lobby for their agenda.

As wealth has concentrated in fewer hands, some of that wealth, often as part of a tax avoidance strategy, flows into the creation of charitable foundations. Since 1980, when disparities in wealth began to accelerate, the number of private foundations has tripled, from 22,088 to more than 76,000 in 2010.[6]

These private foundations, largely controlled by families in the 1 percent, give to a variety of issues and concerns, mostly apolitical. The largest recipients are universities, hospitals, and religious institutions—and the charity dollars are urgently needed. Only a tiny percent, however, estimated at around 3 percent, is given to projects that address poverty alleviation and the root causes of social problems. The largest percentage of contributions reinforces or even perpetuates the unequal status quo.[7]

The game riggers within the 1 percent use charitable foundations as an extension of their advocacy power. Billionaire Steve Forbes formed a tax-exempt think tank to promote himself and his policies in advance of his run for president in 2000. George Soros gives billions through the Open Society Fund to support global development and liberal organizations in the United States.

Using Media Influence to Change the Conversation

The concentration of media ownership is a major factor in shaping the contours of our national debate. The ownership and actions of

News Corporation, Viacom, and other major media outlets are probably more significant in shaping the economy than is money given to politicians.

The 1 percent own a disproportionately large share of media outlets and have an outsized ability to influence the media through public relations and communications firms. This has greatly shaped the national conversation about the existence of inequality and possible solutions. Later in this book, I make the case for a robust role for government action to reduce inequality. Yet public opinion is confused about whether this is a good idea.

Over the last few decades, the 1 percent and Wall Street have funneled billions of dollars to think tanks, communications firms, lobbying groups, and nonprofit charitable organizations that promote the demonization of government as a solution to our common problems. So even at a time when two-thirds of the population is concerned about extreme inequality, there is abundant confusion about whether government action can solve the problem.[8] The invisibility of inequality concerns in the media is a contributing factor to this confusion.

Organizing Others in the 1 Percent and Leveraging Networks

The most engaged rule riggers use their networks, associations, cultural institutions, and connections to other wealthy people and corporate leaders to leverage additional power and influence.

For example, some members of the 1 percent join with others to bundle their donations and have them come from an organized association with an agenda. In one study, 21 percent of the members of the 1 percent sampled had bundled their campaign contributions with those of other donors to increase impact.[9] This really engages the attention of politicians.

Partnering with Wall Street Game Riggers

Individuals in the top 1 percent who are active game riggers are usually linked to corporations connected to Wall Street. As we shall discuss in chapter 5, Wall Street is the 1 percent's institutional home—and the engine of activity that has fueled inequality and economic instability.

Like wealthy individuals, the mega-corporations of Wall Street fund a network of pro-free-market think tanks, research organizations, advocacy groups, and associations such as the U.S. Chamber of Commerce and the Business Roundtable that have armies of lobbyists and public relations firms.

These five uses of influence by a segment of the 1 percent have led to new levels of inequality—and a form of plutocracy rule by a wealthy elite that uses its power to expand its wealth and power.

Profile of a Game Rigger

Perhaps the best case study of using wealth and power to perpetuate wealth and power is the Koch brothers. David and Charles Koch, two brothers who inherited an oil business, are worth an estimated $25 billion each. They use every tool possible to advance their interests—which includes blocking climate change legislation, cutting their taxes, and weakening government regulation.

In addition to active campaign and political issue contributions, they fund an infrastructure of radical libertarian and anti-government organizations, including the Tea Party movement, Americans for Prosperity, and incubators of libertarian thought such as the Mercatus Center at George Mason University.

They've donated hundreds of millions of dollars to right-wing causes over the last decade and convene semiannual gatherings of some of the richest conservatives in the country to leverage money for issue and electoral work. They are currently financing a gigantic database project to expand right-wing organizing and mobilize over $200 million for the 2012 elections.[10]

What makes their use of tax-exempt charitable donations doubly offensive is that taxpayers in the bottom 99 percent indirectly subsidize the Koch brothers and other billionaires who fund pet political projects through tax-exempt charities. Many working-class donors don't itemize their deductions on their taxes, so they don't receive a tax break. But for the wealthy, the charitable deduction is a major incentive for giving and greatly reduces their tax obligations. For every $100 donated by the 1 percent, $33 in revenue is lost to the U.S. Treasury. In other words, the 99 percent matches a third of their donations.[11]

Government Help for the 1 Percent

When the rule riggers in the 1 percent use their substantial influence, what do they get for their efforts? What is their policy agenda and how successful has it been? Below are examples of policies widely advocated by the rule riggers within the top 1 percent.

Low Taxes on Income from Wealth. Capital gains taxes have been greatly reduced over the last several decades, from 39 percent in 1979 to 15 percent in 2011. The 1 percent receive over 80 percent of capital gains income, with the top 0.1 percent receiving over half of capital gains income.[12]

Free Trade to Boost Investors. Free trade policies and treaties have boosted stock prices and enabled companies to pit countries against one another in a race to the bottom in wages, environmental standards, and worker protection. For several decades, free trade treaties have passed the U.S. Congress with bipartisan majorities over the objections of a majority of the population.[13] They have benefited the top 1 percent of shareholders but hurt the 99 percent of wage earners by driving down wages.

Unlimited Inheritances. The federal estate tax is our nation's only levy on inherited wealth. Eliminating this tax, paid only by the 1 percent, remains a major legislative priority for many in Congress. The 1 percent lobbied to phase out the estate tax in 2010. We presently have a diminished estate tax on wealth over $5 million.

Weak Environmental Regulation and Enforcement. The 1 percent has lobbied to weaken environmental regulation and enforcement, blocking responses to the climate crisis to enable extractive industries such as oil and coal to reap short-term windfalls.

Tax Cuts for the Top. The 1 percent has won reductions in top income tax rates. Since 1980, top income tax rates have gone from 50 percent to 35 percent. As described earlier, the 1 percent has seen the percentage of its income paid in taxes decline since the 1950s.

Secret Tax Havens. Expansion of the offshore tax haven system and secrecy jurisdictions enable the 1 percent of companies to hide income and assets and reduce or eliminate their taxes. Lobbying has kept Congress from cracking down.

Subsidies for the Future. Tax subsidies for 1 percent corporations have made it possible not just to avoid taxes but also to get money from taxpayers. General Electric received $3.3 billion in 2010.

The 1 percent has seen their agenda move successfully through the halls of Congress. They've also successfully fended off rule changes they opposed. The 99 percent have not been so fortunate.

4 Life in the 99 Percent

Great accumulations of wealth cannot be justified on the basis
of personal and family security. . . . In the last analysis, such
accumulations amount to the perpetuation of great and undesirable
concentration of control in a relatively few individuals. . . . Such
inherited economic power is as inconsistent with the ideals of this
generation as inherited political power was inconsistent with the
ideals of the generation which established our government.
—Franklin Delano Roosevelt

The bottom 99 percent in the United States represents about 310
million people and over 150 million households.

The bottom 99 percent includes a wide spectrum of people, from
those who are homeless and destitute all the way to relatively affluent
households with a couple of million dollars in wealth. The higher
they are in the 99 percent, the more they have benefited from rule
changes in the economy that propelled the 1 percent. The further
they are from the top, the less they have benefited.

Those in the 99 percent have seen their national share of income
decline from 91 percent in 1976 to 79 percent in 2010.[1] The share of
wealth owned by the bottom 90 percent declined from 19.1 percent
in 1962 to 12.8 percent in 2009.[2] It is worth repeating that during
1983 and 2009, no wealth gains went to the bottom 60 percent of
the U.S. population. In fact, their wealth declined since 1983. Meanwhile, 82 percent of all wealth gains flowed to the richest 5 percent.

The Declining Power of the 99 Percent

Over the last thirty years, as campaign contributions came to trump votes, the 1 percent and Wall Street gained power through their organized lobbying and associations, while the 99 percent and Main Street lost clout.

Those among the 99 percent who organize are less powerful than they were a generation ago. In 1955, over 35 percent of U.S. workers were in a trade union. Unions used their collective-bargaining power and advocated for policies to ensure that a portion of the income and wealth gains of the economy were shared more broadly. In 2011, the proportion of workers in a union plummeted to under 12 percent.[3] This is a dramatic loss in voice and power for wage earners in the 99 percent, most of whom have been ignored by politicians.

Similarly, participation in civic associations and social movements has declined or been rendered invisible by the growing power of Wall Street, corporate PR firms, corporate media, and campaign contributions.[4] (See the section titled "Shifting Power" on page 93.)

The Agenda of the 99 Percent

What is the policy agenda that serves the 99 percent? Polls reflect that most of the population aspires to live in a society with greater equality and economic security. In fact, recent surveys indicate that Americans would prefer to live in a society like Sweden, which has greater equality.[5] Below are examples of policies widely favored by the 99 percent.

More Time for What Matters. Reduced work hours, so we can spend more time with people we love and care for one another. In fact, people are working more hours and have more members of their families in the paid labor force. People today have less free time than previous generations did.

Minimal Economic Security. A minimal social safety net, so people don't have to worry about becoming completely destitute if they lose a job or a spouse, get sick, or simply age. This safety net includes universal health care, affordable housing and transit, an old-age pension (Social Security), and minimal guaranteed income. The effort to pass universal health insurance made modest progress in 2009, but substantive reforms were blocked, largely by the 1 percent of insurance industry corporations that extract tremendous profits from health care.

Quality Education. Strong educational institutions and equal opportunity in education, from early childhood education through quality elementary and secondary schooling and all the way to affordable or free college education. Many students graduate from college today with huge debt burdens.

Putting Children First. Policies that put children first in terms of access to effective health care, good child care, healthful food, and quality education. Instead, more children live in poverty than ever before and the government is cutting back on Head Start and other funding for children and families.

Aid to Jobless. Help for the unemployed, especially in a severe economic downturn with an unemployment rate of over 9 percent. Instead, major interventions that would have boosted employment have been blocked, and Congress has come close to failing to extend unemployment benefits for the long-term unemployed.

Poverty Elimination. Reduction in the number of people living below the poverty line. Instead, poverty rates have risen in the last decade, with child poverty at its highest level since the United States started measuring this statistic in 1962.

It's not that there is no political support for the agenda of the 99 percent, but consider the lack of progress compared to the agenda of the 1 percent discussed in chapter 3.

The agenda of the 99 percent has been trumped by that of the 1 percent. A growing number of politicians have become advocates for a policy program that predominantly serves the 1 percent. They argue that policies such as tax cuts for the 1 percent are good for the economy, create jobs, and so on. And they block policy changes that would benefit the 99 percent, arguing that this constitutes big government and is unaffordable. But the results are growing levels of inequality that, we will argue shortly, undermine economic health and well being for everyone.

Diversity within the 99 Percent

One of the legitimate objections to the 99 to 1 framework is that it glosses over some substantial differences within the 99 percent, including the diversity of race, the experience of poverty and destitution, and the wide disparities of opportunity that exist.

Obviously, there is a massive gulf between someone in the top 95 to 99 percent who owns two houses and has a retirement fund and someone in the bottom 20 percent who has no savings, has poor health care, and lives in a crime-filled neighborhood. Owning a home, having savings, and having access to higher education, recreation, and leisure leads to longer life expectancy, less stress, and greater happiness.[6]

Someone in the top 30 percent experiences day-to-day life in different ways than someone in the one in four households in the United States that has zero or negative net worth and someone in the 37 percent of households that have a net worth of less than $12,000.[7] These are families that have no cushion to absorb economic shocks or setbacks.

Within the 99 percent, there are enormous racial wealth disparities. The median net worth of white households in 2009 was $113,149, more than twenty times the median net worth of African American

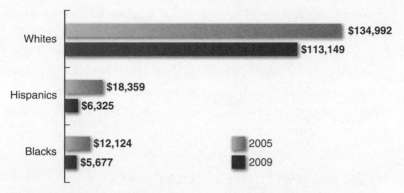

Figure 9. Racial wealth disparities have worsened in the aftermath of the 2008 economic meltdown. Source: Pew Research Center tabulations of Survey of Income and Program Participation data.

households ($5,677) and eighteen times that of Hispanic households ($6,325). The racial wealth gap widened between 2007 and 2010, as households of color lost trillions in home equity in the aftermath of the subprime mortgage crisis.[8]

In 2005, prior to the implosion of home values, white households had eleven times the median net worth of African American households and seven times the net worth of Hispanic households. The collapse of home values hurt everyone, but not equally. Between 2005 and 2009, the median net worth of whites declined by 16 percent, a colossal hit in terms of wealth. Households of color, however, were walloped. Hispanic households saw their wealth plummet by 66 percent, and blacks witnessed a 53 percent drop.

These disparities can be explained only by the multigenerational legacy of racial discrimination in mortgage lending, employment, and access to capital for enterprise development. These barriers prevented millions of households from getting on the wealth-building train. Meanwhile, whites in the years after World War II experienced what Ira Katznelson called "white affirmative action," a set of racially discriminatory wealth-building programs that boosted the rates of homeownership, savings, and college graduation among white households.[9]

To talk about the 99 percent is not to ignore the reality of class and racial difference in America. Life is class-coded in dozens of ways that affect health, education, and quality of life. In an economically polarized society, class differences are infused with even greater power and meaning.

The Common Ground of the 99 Percent

In spite of the obvious diversity within the 99 percent, the 99 to 1 framework is a useful window into our changing economy and power structure. Seeing the important distinctions within the 99 percent should not obscure what the members of this group share. The economy has been organized largely to benefit this richest 1 percent.

Politically, it is important that the 99 percent see that they have some important common ground, rather than be peeled into a hundred subgroupings. Historically, we have made little progress addressing inequality because different factions of the 99 percent have been pitted against one another in policy fights.

For example, historically the working poor and working class have been encouraged to resent the rock-bottom poor (those in the lowest 20 percent). And the middle class—those in the 30th to 70th percentiles of income and wealth—have been encouraged to identify their aspirations with the affluent and very wealthy and view their interests as wholly distinct from those of the working class. This in part explains why middle-class people support tax cuts for the 1 percent.

The economic implosion that began in 2006—including the evaporation of $8 trillion in housing wealth—is a powerful example of how almost everyone in the 99 percent was touched, albeit differently, by the same destructive economic policies.

What's important about this moment—and the 99 percent movement—is that it can help us understand how the real engine of inequality comes from this super-rich class and the Wall Street inequality machine. A spotlight is being shined on how the 1 percent deploys its wealth and power to preserve and expand its bankroll and privileges.

If the 99 percent viewed themselves as an interest group and a political force, it could have huge implications for the future of our economy and society. And if the 99 percent would stick together—and win over allies within the 1 percent—then we would have a shot at changing the rules of the economy in a way that benefits everyone, not just the few.

5 The Wall Street Inequality Machine

The priority of the money system shifted from funding real investment for building community wealth to funding financial games designed solely to enrich Wall Street without the burden of producing anything of value.
—David Korten

When we talk about the 1 percent, it is tempting to personalize it, envisioning individual millionaires and specific people in the bottom 99 percent. This is reinforced by the photographs that thousands of people have posted on websites with their "I am the 99 percent" stories.

But, as we've discussed, a key explanation for the lopsided distribution of wealth is how the 1 percent teams up with leaders of large transnational corporations in the United States and the rest of the world. In fact, many of the leaders of large transnational corporations are members of the predatory, rule-rigging 1 percent. This corporate 1 percent owns a gigantic percentage of the globe's private assets and transmits it though ownership flows to shareholders, most of whom are in the top 1 percent of individuals.

As with the top 1 percent of individuals, the 1 percent of corporations is diverse. The transnational corporations that exercise disproportionate influence include the roughly 300 corporations that make up the leadership of lobbying groups such as the U.S. Chamber of Commerce and the Business Roundtable.

Corporations don't exist apart from people. They are human-created legal constructs. Corporations don't make decisions and lobby for rule changes. People who run corporations—CEOs and top managers—make decisions and profit royally from them.

The CEOs and corporate top 1 percent constitute the Wall Street inequality machine, the central organizing locus that advocates for rule changes tilted in favor of the 1 percent. Like the individual 1 percent, these top corporate managers have many tools at their disposal for shaping the economic rules and culture of the society, only theirs are even more powerful. These tools include armies of lobbyists, bundled campaign contributions, powerful communications and advertising agencies, and more.

The term "Wall Street" both describes the finance capital sector of the economy and symbolizes the corporate 1 percent, the several thousand global companies that dwarf in size some countries. Centered on Wall Street are the financial firms and banks that wield a dizzying amount of wealth and clout. These include Goldman Sachs, Morgan Stanley, JPMorgan Chase, Wells Fargo, Bank of America, Citigroup, Barclays, Deutsche Bank, Credit Suisse, and UBS.

Simon Johnson, a professor of entrepreneurship at the MIT Sloan School of Management, testified that the six largest bank holding companies in the United States "currently have assets valued at just

1. Bank of America Corp.	$2.264 trillion
2. J.P. Morgan Chase & Co.	$2.246 trillion
3. Citigroup, Inc.	$1.957 trillion
4. Wells Fargo & Co.	$1.260 trillion
5. Goldman Sachs Group, Inc.	$937 billion
6. Morgan Stanley	$831 billion

Figure 10. Too big to fail? The six biggest U.S. bank holding companies have assets valued at 63 percent of the U.S. gross domestic product. Source: National Information Center, Federal Reserve. Values as of September 30, 2011.

over 63 percent of [U.S.] GDP," citing figures for the fourth quarter of 2010. "This is up from around 55 percent of GDP before the economic crisis (e.g., 2006) and no more than 17 percent of GDP in 1995."[1]

Not only do these Wall Street financial firms exercise tremendous financial power, but also, by virtue of the enormous sums of money and profits generated by this sector, they exert significant political power through campaign contributions, lobbying clout, and the funding of research and advocacy that advance their interests. The financial, insurance, and real estate (FIRE) sectors are the largest contributors to political campaigns and employ thousands of lobbyists, several for each elected member of Congress.[2]

Wall Street and the financial sector within it have profited handsomely from their ability to rig the rules, capturing an ever larger share of global wealth and profits. Paralleling the thirty-year rise of extreme inequality, Wall Street financial firms expanded dramatically; by 2007, an estimated 40 percent of corporate profits came from the financial sector, up from 20 percent in the 1960s. In the aftermath of the 2008 economic meltdown, the proportion of profits attributed to the financial industry has declined to roughly 30 percent.[3]

A large percent of the total income of the 1 percent, in turn, is associated with this rise of the financial sector, which is the major employer at the top end of the income ladder. According to the Economic Policy Institute, the "share of national income attributable to compensation and profits in the corporate financial sector more than doubled between 1973 and 2007, to 7 percent. In 2010, this translated into an additional $547 billion claimed by the financial sector—even though there is little evidence of added value to the real economy—the economy of actual goods and services."[4]

Within the corporate 1 percent, some companies are just too large and powerful. A handful of global corporations have annual revenues that surpass the gross domestic product of entire countries. In terms

Figure 11. Some corporations have annual sales in excess of the gross domestic product of entire countries.

of revenue, General Electric is bigger than New Zealand and would rank as the world's fifty-second-biggest country. ExxonMobil is bigger than Thailand. Walmart is bigger than Norway and would rank as the twenty-fifth-biggest country.[5]

The lobbying agenda of the corporate 1 percent is similar to the agenda of the top 1 percent of wealthy individuals. It includes corporate deregulation, weakening of environmental laws, special tax treatment and loopholes, weakening of worker health and safety rules, and blocking expansion of public health and food safety oversight.

Through their virtual lock on the U.S. Congress, the top 1 percent of large corporations have effectively captured our democratic system. The Supreme Court's *Citizens United* decision has unleashed additional corporate money and power (See the *Citizens United* and Corporate Power boxed feature on page 113).

Corporations and the CEOs Who Lead Them

Commanding the corporate 1 percent—and personally overseeing the work of the Wall Street inequality machine—are the CEOs of several thousand of the world's largest companies.

Within this elite group are several hundred "imperial CEOs," who operate largely free of accountability to shareholders and even the company's board of directors.[6] They receive huge compensation for their work, often whether or not their company is profitable or making good long-term decisions. In 2010, average CEO pay for an S&P 500 company was $10.8 million, a 27 percent increase over 2009. The ratio of CEO compensation to average U.S. worker pay is 325 to 1, up from 42 to 1 in 1980.[7]

The root problem with CEO pay is the underlying system of incentives. Current compensation practices encourage a very short-term outlook and reward short-term decisions that goose immediate profits over long-term strategies that foster healthy, durable, built-to-last companies. Roger Martin, dean of the University of Toronto business school, has blasted the current U.S. compensation system of "profit maximization" that encourages CEOs to game the system. In this structure, "customers become marks to be exploited, employees become disposable cogs," and shareholders see their equity values plummet.[8]

There is a perverse incentive, for example, to use a corporation's power and influence to distort the regulatory environment it operates in. For example, of the 100 highest-paid CEOs in 2010, 25 took home more compensation than their company paid in federal income taxes. Twenty of these companies spent more on lobbying lawmakers than they paid in corporate taxes, and eighteen gave more in money in bundled contributions to political candidates than they paid the IRS in taxes.[9]

Another perverse incentive is that companies lower their tax bills by overcompensating their executives. The higher CEO paychecks soar, the larger the amount corporations can deduct off their taxes, because compensation is a business expense. Here are a few examples of champion rule riggers:

- The CEO of International Paper Company, John Faraci, pocketed $12.3 million in pay in 2010. He led the company in its congressional lobbying efforts to have an old wood-pulp by-product, "black liquor," classified as a biofuel and eligible for government subsidies and tax refunds.[10] This help cut International Paper's tax bill by $379 million in 2009 and $40 million in 2010—nearly 9 percent of the company's global revenue.[11]
- Jeffrey Immelt, CEO of General Electric, was paid $15.2 million in 2010. GE wins the gold medal in tax avoidance gymnastics, bringing in $3.3 billion in tax subsidies and refunds in 2010, despite more than $5 billion in U.S. profits. An exposé by the *New York Times* on GE's "extraordinary success" in lowering its tax bill found the company engaged in "an aggressive strategy that mixes fierce lobbying for tax breaks and innovative accounting that enables it to concentrate its profits offshore."[12]

The 2008 economic meltdown was fueled by hundreds of these short-term take-the-money-and-run stories and a CEO compensation system that encourages such behavior.

The 99 Percent of Business

The bottom 99 percent of business is wholly a different creature. The business 99 percent are mostly domestic companies and small businesses rooted in localities where management and employees are more accountable to their communities rather than focused solely on maximizing financial returns to absentee stakeholders.

There are, of course, low-road fly-by-night enterprises within the bottom 99 percent that squeeze employees and make decisions based on short-term gains. But the durable ones, those that stay around for years, consider their employees as assets, not expenses to be eliminated. They are concerned about the livelihoods of employees rather than eliminating labor costs by outsourcing.

The business 99 percent typically pay their fair share of taxes, lacking some of the tools for tax dodging available to transnational companies. They populate local chambers of commerce and small business networks. The smaller businesses, those with fewer than 500 employees, are the engines of job creation and hiring in the current economy, creating over 60 percent of all private sector jobs. One Bureau of Labor Studies report stated, "Small firms with fewer than 500 employees accounted for 64 percent of the net new jobs created between 1993 and 2008." More than two-thirds of these jobs stemmed from business expansions, with the remaining net employment coming from the balance of new start-ups minus firm closures.[13]

Research reveals that new entrepreneurial ventures provide a major boost to employment, and therefore to the economy. Firms less than five years old are the source of much of the net job generation, and without start-ups, overall net job change might have been negative in most of the years since 1980.[14] During the recession economy of 2008 and 2009, businesses with fewer than five employees were the only ones that had a net increase in employment.[15]

Because smaller companies are invested in their communities, they tend to focus on long-term, shared prosperity. They may be more likely to advocate for public investments in the education and infrastructure that their employees, suppliers, and customers rely on. They also tend to take seriously their roles as stewards of the natural environment.[16]

Smaller businesses are also acutely aware that they operate in a competitive environment. Most understand that they will lose if they engage in a race to the bottom with super-sized, global companies. So they have figured out niches where they can succeed by staying small. Their approach offers a potential model in which smaller businesses are not only the engines of the economy but also key participants in steering the economy toward a more humane and sustainable future.

Companies That Are Built to Last Versus Built to Loot

The business model of the game-rigging corporate 1 percent is dramatically different from that of the business 99 percent. Companies in the business 99 percent are more "built to last," a designation from business journalist Jim Collins used to describe companies interested in long-term growth and profitability through slow and careful decisions and respectful relationships with all stakeholders.

A dangerously large segment of the corporate 1 percent, however, pursues a different business model. Such companies are "built to loot." Their focus is on short-term profit grabbing, and they routinely shift costs off their balance sheets and onto society, localities, the environment, or workers.

The incentives within the competitive global corporate arena drive this behavior. These companies must compete by using their global status and subsidiaries to avoid accountability and responsibility. They pit countries and communities against one another in a race to lower standards.

Seven Ways That Built-to-Loot Corporations Have Rigged the System to Worsen Inequality

Treat Employees as Disposable. These companies view labor as a cost, not an asset. They drive down labor costs by eliminating any positions with security and benefits and shift to consultants, contingent part-time workers, and outsourcing firms both in the United States and abroad.

Game the Rules on Global Trade. Companies lobby for trade rules that boost corporate rights at the expense of worker rights, privileging global companies over Main Street businesses.

Lobby for Subsidies. Companies lobby Congress to create subsidies and targeted tax breaks. Corporate lobbying pays off. The financial services sector received 16.8 percent of all federal tax subsidies between 2008 and 2010. The bank Wells Fargo topped the list of 280 U.S. corporations, receiving $18 billion in tax breaks over three years.

Tilt the Playing Field through Deregulation. Companies advocate for lower standards in every possible arena, pressing for deregulation of environmental standards, labor rules, requirements for community notification, or any other form of disclosure.

Control the Conversation: Media Ownership. The concentration of media ownership in the corporate 1 percent narrows and cheapens public discourse. In 1983, about fifty media conglomerates controlled more than half of all broadcast media (including newspapers, magazines, radio, music, publishing, and film) in the country. Today, six transnational media conglomerates dominate the American mass media landscape.

Dodge Taxes: Pass the Bill. Get someone else to pay your bills for the public services and market environment that you enjoy. (See the boxed feature on page 58.)

Skew Global Investment Rules. Global investment agreements have benefited the corporate 1 percent and encouraged further capital flows into the unproductive speculative sector. Transnational companies can move money around through cross-border flows that avoid oversight and accountability.

Corporate Tax Dodgers Hurt Responsible Business

A 2011 study by Citizens for Tax Justice found that 280 of the most profitable U.S. corporations had dodged taxes on half of their profits over the previous three years. Thirty of the companies paid no taxes and received substantial subsidies between 2008 and 2010, despite combined pre-tax profits of $160 billion, and seventy-eight paid no federal corporate income tax during at least one of the three years.

The average effective rate for all 280 companies between 2008 and 2010 was 18.5 percent, far less than the statutory corporate income tax rate of 35 percent. "These 280 corporations received a total of nearly $223 billion in tax subsidies," observed Robert McIntyre, director at Citizens for Tax Justice and lead author of the report. "This is wasted money that could have gone to protect Medicare, create jobs and cut the deficit."[17]

These tax gymnastics create a fundamentally unfair and unlevel playing field between the corporate 1 percent and the smaller business 99 percent. For example, Amazon.com paid a federal corporate tax rate of 7.9 percent on its $1.8 billion in profits between 2008 and 2010. It also dodges massive amounts of state and local sales taxes, which their local competitors must collect from costumers. Local independent booksellers and Main Street retailers have been decimated by Amazon.com's huge tax advantages.

Even companies within the 1 percent compete unfairly. FedEx paid a tax rate of less than 1 percent during the period 2008 to 2010, while its unionized competitor, UPS, paid 24.1 percent.

6 How Inequality Wrecks Everything We Care About

The reality is that U.S. society is polarizing and its social arteries are hardening. The sumptuousness and bleakness of the respective lifestyles of rich and poor represents a scale of difference in opportunity and wealth that is almost medieval—and a standing offense to the American expectation that everyone has the opportunity for life, liberty and happiness.
—Will Hutton (b. 1951)

Inequality is wrecking the world. Not just poverty, which is destroying the lives of billions of people around the planet, but also inequality— the accelerating gap between the 99 percent and the 1 percent.

The Inequality Death Spiral

According to research in dozens of disciplines, the extreme disparities of wealth and power corrode our democratic system and public trust. They lead to a breakdown in civic cohesion and social solidarity, which in turn leads to worsened health outcomes.

Inequality undercuts social mobility and has disastrous effects on economic stability and growth. The notion of a "death spiral" may sound dramatic, but it captures the dynamic and reinforcing aspects of inequality. And these inequalities were a major contributing factor to the 1929 and 2008 economic downturns. What follows is the case against inequality.

Inequality Wrecks Our Democracy and Civic Life

Inequality is disenfranchising us, diminishing our vote at the ballot box and our voice in the public square. As dollars of the 1 percent displace the votes of the 99 percent as the currency of politics, the 1 percent wins. Not every time, but enough so that the tilt continues toward the agenda of the 1 percent.

The money of the 1 percent dominates our campaign finance system, even after efforts at reform. To run for U.S. Senate—or to win additional terms in the Senate after being elected—politicians must raise an estimated $15,000 a day in campaign contributions. To do this efficiently, politicians have to spend a lot of time courting people in the 1 percent, attending $1,000-a-plate fund-raising dinners and listening to their concerns and agenda. This means less time shaking hands in front of the Costco or Cracker Barrel. We all respond to the people we are surrounded by, and politicians are no different.

Elections do matter. Politicians care about votes on Election Day, and they campaign for those votes and work to get supporters to the polls. But candidates for the U.S. Congress know that every other day of the year they have to think about money.

The corporate 1 percent dominates the lobbying space around federal and state policies. In the last thirty years, the ranks of official lobbyists have exploded. In 1970, there were five registered lobbyists for every one of the 535 members of Congress. Today there are twenty-two lobbyists for every member.[1]

Who lobbies for the 99 percent? There are impressive organizations out there, such as Public Citizen and the Children's Defense Fund, that stand up, wave their arms, and say, "Hey, what about the 99 percent?" But they are severely underresourced, outgunned, and outmaneuvered by the organized 1 percent.

Inequality Makes Us Sick

The medical researchers have said it. And now a growing body of public health research is arriving at the same conclusion: inequality is making us sick.

The more inequality grows between the 1 percent and the 99 percent, the less healthy we are. Unequal communities have greater rates of heart disease, asthma, mental illness, cancer, and other morbid illnesses.

Of course, poverty contributes to all kinds of bad health outcomes. But research shows that you are better off in a low-income community with greater equality than you are in a community with a higher income but more extreme inequalities.

Counties and countries with lower incomes but less inequality have better health outcomes. They have lower infant mortality rates, longer life expectancy, and lower incidences of all kinds of diseases. Counties with higher average incomes but greater disparities between rich and poor have the opposite indicators. They are less healthy places to live.[2]

Why is this so? According to British health researcher Richard Wilkinson, communities with less inequality have stronger "social cohesion," more cultural limits on unrestrained individualism, and more effective networks of mutual aid and caring. "The individualism and values of the market are restrained by a social morality," Wilkinson writes. The existence of more social capital "lubricates the workings of the whole society and economy. There are fewer signs of antisocial aggressiveness, and society appears more caring."[3]

Inequality Tears Our Communities Apart

Extreme inequalities of wealth rip our communities apart with social divisions and distrust, leading to an erosion of social cohesion and solidarity. The 1 percent and the 99 percent today don't just live on opposite sides of the tracks—they occupy parallel universes.

New research shows that we're becoming more polarized by class and race in terms of where we live. A 2011 report based on U.S. Census data notes, "As overall income inequality grew in the last four decades, high- and low-income families have become increasingly less likely to live near one another. Mixed income neighborhoods have grown rarer, while affluent and poor neighborhoods have grown much more common."[4] As this distance widens, it is harder for people to feel like they are in the same boat.

High levels of inequality lead to the construction of physical walls. In many parts of the world, the members of the 1 percent reside in gated communities, surrounded by security systems and bodyguards. More than 9 million households in the United States live behind walls in gated communities, similar to the statistics in polarized societies such as Mexico and Brazil. Over a third of new housing starts in the southern United States are in gated communities.[5]

The relationship between the 1 percent and the 99 percent is characterized by fear, distance, misunderstanding, distrust, and class and racial antagonisms. As a result, there is less caring and a greater amount of individualistic behavior. Part of how people express care is support for public investments in health infrastructure and prevention that benefit everyone. As societies grow unequal, support for such investments declines.

Solidarity is characterized by people taking responsibility for one another and caring for neighbors. But for solidarity to happen, people must know one another and have institutions that transcend differences in class, culture, and race. In communities with great inequality, these institutions don't exist and solidarity is weakened.

Inequality Erodes Social Mobility and Equal Opportunity

Inequality undermines the cherished value of equality of opportunity and social mobility. Intergenerational mobility is the possibility of shifting up or down the income ladder relative to your parents' status. In a mobile society, your economic circumstances are not defined or limited by the economic origins of your family.

For many decades, economists argued that inequality in the United States was the price we paid for a dynamic economy with social mobility.[6] We didn't want to be like Canada or those northern European economies, economists would argue, with their rigid class systems and lack of mobility.

But here's the bad news: Canada and those European nations—with their social safety nets and progressive tax policies—are now more mobile than U.S. society. Research across the industrialized OECD countries has found that Canada, Australia, and the Nordic countries (Denmark, Norway, Sweden, and Finland) are among the most mobile. There is a strong correlation between social mobility and policies that redistribute income and wealth through taxation. The United States is now among the *least* mobile of industrialized countries in terms of earnings.[7]

Inequality Erodes Public Services

The 99 percent depends on the existence of a robust commonwealth of public and community institutions. As Bill Gates Sr., the father of the founder of Microsoft, wrote,

> The ladder of opportunity for America's middle class depends on strong and accessible public educational institutions, libraries, state parks and municipal pools. And for America's poor, the ladder of opportunity also includes access to affordable health care, quality public transportation, and childcare assistance.[8]

Historically, during times of great inequality, there is a disinvestment in the commonwealth.[9] There is less support provided for education, affordable housing, public health care, and other pillars of a level playing field. By contrast, in 1964, a time of relative equality, there was greater concern about poverty; in fact, we launched the War on Poverty to further reduce disadvantage.

Today, as the 1 percent delinks from our communities, it privatizes the services it needs. This leads to two bad outcomes. First, because the 1 percent does not depend on commonwealth services, it would rather not pay for them. They often prefer tax cuts and limited government, which leave them more of their money to spend on privatized services.

Second, the quality of life for the 99 percent suffers when the wealthy don't have a personal stake in maintaining quality public services. As we've seen, the 1 percent has tremendous clout. Its members have the ear of elected officials, command over charitable dollars, dominance of media ownership, and networking connections that are sometimes called "social capital." In a democratic society, good government and strong public institutions require civic engagement by everyone. But when those with the biggest amount of political power, largest number of connections, and greatest capacity don't have a stake, a cycle of disinvestment occurs.

The cycle of disinvestment begins when public services start to deteriorate after the withdrawal of tax dollars and the participation of the powerful. For example, if someone doesn't use the neighborhood public swimming pool because he or she belongs to a private club or spends summers at a private beach house, that person doesn't have a stake in ensuring that the public swimming pool is open all summer, clean and well maintained, and staffed with qualified lifeguards. When services deteriorate and the powerful no longer participate, it leads to a decline in political support and resources, which in turn leads to a cycle of further disinvestment.

This lack of stake is even more visible in terms of public education, where the withdrawal of the 1 percent and even the top 30 percent of families has contributed to severe disinvestment in some school districts. This triggers a vicious circle of budget cuts, stakeholders pulling out, and declining public support for education.

The cycle of disinvestment accelerates when it becomes rational to abandon public and community services if one can afford to do so. Those who can get out do so, in a rush-to-the-exits moment. Families in the 99 percent work extra hard to privatize the services they need until there is a wholesale withdrawal from the public sphere.

If you can't depend on the bus to get to work, you buy a car. If you can't rely on the local public schools to educate your child, then you stretch to pay for private schools. If you can't depend on the lifeguards to show up at the public pool, then you join the private pool. If you can't depend on the police to protect your neighborhood, you hire a private security service or move to a gated community. The cycle of disinvestment continues and the costs of privatized services rise, trapping the remaining families in poor schools and neighborhoods lacking services.

Inequality Undermines Economic Growth

Remember the last time in history that the 1 percent had such a large share of the wealth pie? It was 1929, the eve of the Great Depression. Economic historians argue that this was not a coincidence. Too much inequality contributes to economic instability.

The corollary is that periods of shared prosperity have greater economic growth and stability. The period after World War II, 1947 to 1977, is often cited as a case study of a high-growth and high-equality period.

Making such comparisons is fraught with danger—we're not just comparing apples and oranges, we're comparing bicycles and dump trucks. The period after World War II was unprecedented in terms of the dominant and unrivaled role the United States played in the global economy. But international comparative data that look at inequality and economic performance reinforce this story. More-equal societies do better on most indicators.

The conventional wisdom, espoused in the 1960s by economists such as Arthur Okun of the Brookings Institution, was that there was a trade-off between growth and equity: policies that increased equality would slow economic growth, and aggressive pro-growth policies would worsen inequality. But this thinking is now being turned on its head.

Research by the International Monetary Fund (IMF) and the National Bureau of Economic Research point to the fact that more-equal societies have stronger rates of growth, experience longer economic expansions, and are quicker to recover from economic downturns. According to Jonathan Ostry, an economist at the IMF, trends toward unequal income in the United States mean that future economic expansions will be just one-third as long as they were in the 1960s, prior to the widening of the income divide. Less-equal societies are more vulnerable to both financial crises and political instability.[10]

In volatile markets, investors become gun-shy, even those in the 1 percent. When they perceive that financial markets are rigged in favor of insiders and the politically connected, they take their money somewhere else. "You're going to lose a generation of investors," observed Barry Ritholtz, an investor researcher with Fusion IQ. "And that's how you end up with a 25-year bear market. That's the risk if people start to think there is no economic justice."[11]

Many economists have drawn parallels between 1929 on the eve of the Great Depression and the 2008 economic meltdown. Raghuram Rajan, a former chief economist for the IMF, argues that both depressions were preceded by periods of extreme inequality. In his book *Fault Lines: How Hidden Fractures Still Threaten the World Economy*, Rajan observes that during the decade prior to both economic downturns, the 1 percent captured a gigantic percentage of income gains and wages were stagnant for the majority of Americans. Meanwhile, government policies and private corporate practices encouraged easy access to credit and borrowing among the poor and middle classes. Household debt nearly doubled during both periods.[12]

Did inequality play a role in the 2008 economic meltdown? The next chapter takes a closer look at this important question.

7 How Wealth Inequality Crashed the Economy

An economy so dependent on the spending of a few is also prone to great booms and busts. The rich splurge and speculate when their savings are doing well. But when the values of their assets tumble, they pull back. That can lead to wild gyrations. Sound familiar? It's no mere coincidence that over the last century the top earners' share of the nation's total income peaked in 1928 and 2007—the two years just preceding the biggest downturns.
—Robert Reich (b. 1946)

There are many theories about what triggered the 2008 economic meltdown. These explanations focus on bad actors such as the large banks and financial firms, the unregulated "shadow" financial sector, and unethical subprime mortgage pushers.[1]

But there is a missing lens to the story, one that shows how the economic meltdown was caused by excessive income and wealth inequality. The two triggers were consumption by the 99 percent based on borrowing rather than real wage growth, and reckless financial speculation by the 1 percent.

Ingredient 1: Consumption Based on Borrowing, Not Real Wage Growth

Real wages for the bottom 80 percent of households have remained relatively stagnant since the late 1970s. People survived these stagnant

Figure 12. Personal savings rate fell dramatically before 2008 and has rebounded slightly since then. Source: Bureau of Economic Analysis, National Income and Product Accounts, Table 2.1, Personal Income and Its Disposition, line 34.

wages by working more hours, bringing more family members into the paid labor force, and borrowing more, thanks to easy access to credit. This put enormous stresses on many working families as they got caught on a work-consume-borrow treadmill. But for many, this was the only way to attain or maintain a middle-class standard of living.

Most households stopped being able to save. In 1980, the savings rate—the share of people's income saved after expenses—was 11 percent. By 2007, the U.S. savings rate had plummeted to less than 2 percent, meaning people were earning only slightly more than they were spending.

Did things appear different? With a median income of roughly $50,000, many people in the United States were living with little surplus. That said, the parking lots at the mall and the Applebee's restaurant were full. The rising middle class bought new cars, teenagers got smartphones, and families took expensive vacations. These feats of consumption were not a reflection of rising wages. In some cases, increased spending was the result of two or three incomes. But most purchasing was made possible by families taking on more debt. Consumer debt—both credit card and home equity loans—escalated during the decade prior to 2008. The total amount of credit card debt exploded, thanks in part to aggressive "debt pushing." In 2006, there were 6 billion credit card solicitations sent out.[2] The majority of home financing was for second mortgages, not new home acquisitions. Access to easy credit was the drug that enabled millions to live beyond their means.

Exploding consumer debt was worsened by a shift in the culture, as extensive borrowing became more socially sanctioned. The debt pushers contributed to this, advertising cheap credit and peddling home equity loans as the new normal.

Overwork and debt masked the reality of falling and stagnant wages. If you and your neighbors could still acquire a flat-screen TV and take a Caribbean vacation, then it was hard to feel constrained. But these trends were fundamentally unstable. Underlying these indicators was a growing credit card and housing mortgage bubble. Think of the sound track from the movie *Jaws* as a shark creeps up on the unsuspecting swimmer.

The entire economy was humming, but it wasn't based on healthy wage growth and shared prosperity. The consumption engine driving the economic boom between 2000 and 2008 was based on borrowing, not real wage increases.

So when the economy seized up in 2008 and access to easy credit ground to a halt, so did the consumption engine. Millions of people lost their jobs or a significant household income. But they also lost the borrowing lifeline that had eased the gap between inadequate income and spending. Without debt-driven consumer demand, the entire economy froze.

Extremely unequal wages and income contributed to the collapse of consumer buying power. If consumption had been based on a foundation of healthy wage growth, the situation would have been considerably less volatile.

Ingredient Two: Financial Speculation

The dynamic of debt-based consumption was bad enough. But there was another way that inequality contributed to crashing the economy. At the top of the economic pyramid, those in the top 1 percent were doing their part by taking part in risky gambling. Unfortunately, the gambling was not confined to a casino, where the losses could be contained, but took place at the heart of our whole economy.

In 2007, the richest 1 percent owned 36.5 percent of all the private wealth in the United States and over 42.4 percent of all financial assets. Part of this estimated $20 trillion in wealth was in the form of land, houses, artwork, jewelry, private jets, and other private property. But an enormous fraction of it was in the form of stocks, bonds, and ownership stakes in the world's corporations.

The 99 percent, when they have money to invest, look to banks, bonds, and mutual funds. But almost everyone in the 1 percent has investment professionals who advise them about allocating their invested wealth. So imagine for a moment that you're a member of the 1 percent, with $200 million in wealth, and I'm your trusted investment advisor. It's sometime between 2000 and 2007.

I explain that a typical asset allocation strategy is to park a portion of your wealth in stable investments that are a bulwark against serious market downturns. These include insured deposits in banks and credit unions and bonds backed by local, state, or federal governments. This guarantees that you will always be rich, even in tough times. The problem, I explain, is that these have relatively low rates of return. In fact, in 2005, we're talking 2–3 percent returns. In other words, real snoozers.

I suggest taking another portion of your $200 million and investing in some long-term growth equities—companies that have been around for a long time. These include Ford, General Motors, and General Electric, the "blue chip" or seemingly stable companies. But it's the same problem again: very boring and modest returns on investment, maybe 5–6 percent.

With another portion of your funds, we'll start to increase risk and return, looking for a diversified mixture of small- and large-capitalization new companies outside the stock market. These are more interesting and have the potential for higher returns, in the 7–10 percent range.

Now we pause and take a deep breath. Our hearts start to beat a little faster in anticipation of what comes next. Up until now, we've pursued the investment strategy that the super-rich have employed for decades—diversified, sensible, a nice blend of risk and return. We will tweak it based on your age and special needs, but it's a tried-and-true approach.

There is, however, a new class of investments that are generating very high returns. You're smiling because this is what brought you in my door. These new investment vehicles are complicated but highly lucrative—dazzling returns of 10 or 15 percent. Some funds have even had 20 percent returns for five years in a row.

To get those returns, however, we have to make speculative, high-risk investments. These include investments in hedge funds, derivatives, and credit default swaps—some of the financial innovations that some very smart young fellows on Wall Street have designed. These are not investments in the "real economy," in which firms make actual things or provide services that people use. Rather, these are ways to place financial bets on the movement of money and markets. The question for you is, how much are you willing to risk?

Think about your $200 million. If all you had was $20 million, you would be able to live a very wonderful life, meet all your material needs, and guard against most possible problems. You might not be able to buy genuine love or eternal life, though you'll probably live longer. You'll be able to go to the Mayo Clinic for whatever medical need you have and enjoy every luxury the planet has to offer. With another $20 million, you will be able to provide the same to your progeny.

So, setting aside that $40 million, you have $160 million you're willing to gamble with. Wouldn't it be fun to keep score and watch it multiply? It is, after all, mostly just numbers on a page or screen. So we allocate a large portion—let's say $80 million—to the new financial instruments.

Now imagine this same conversation playing out in the wood-paneled offices of the 1 percent all across the planet between 1998 and 2007. As a result, huge amounts of wealth shifted into the speculative market.

The speculative funds of the top 1 percent are merged with additional trillions of dollars in sovereign wealth funds—the colossal piles of wealth generated by Middle Eastern oil profits and Chinese exports and held by central governments. Add to this the trillions in cash accumulated by the world's corporate 1 percent—banks, insurance companies such as AIG, and the finance arms of corporations such as General Electric. That totals trillions of dollars of wealth looking for a home—not in sleepy investments in the real economy, which are incapable of generating such large returns, but in the casino-like speculative economy.

Wall Street drove this process by seeking more and more high-risk deals. One of their favorites was high-interest mortgage debt, known as subprime mortgages. Investment banks and brokers such as Morgan Stanley, Citigroup, and Bank of America called up mortgage lenders and people who bundled mortgages together and said, "Bring us more of those high-return, high-risk deals!" So trillions of dollars flowed into the shadow financial sector—and the deals became more and more delinked from the fundamentals of the real economy.

By 2007, the speculative bubbles had grown, not just in the housing market but also in other sectors of the economy. Commodity futures rose, pushing up the cost of foodstuffs and triggering food riots across the world.[3] Speculation in oil futures drove up the cost of oil, and a gallon of gas during the summer of 2008 topped $4 a gallon. Americans spent hundreds of billions of dollars more on gas in 2008 than they did the previous year.[4] Funds that could have financed a transition to a green economy went to the oil industry, which enjoyed unprecedented profits—in 2008, ExxonMobil set records with profits of $45.2 billion.

Tick, tick, tick. Kaboom!

The extreme inequalities of wealth—stagnant wages and speculative activity—brought the economy to its knees. And here's the bad news: it hasn't stopped. As long as the 1 percent has excess money to bet with, they will continue seeking speculative investments.

Too bad it's not a game in a casino. Unfortunately, it's a very costly game. And the people paying the price with ruined lives are not in the 1 percent.

8 The Sleeping 99 Percent Giant Wakes Up

A true revolution of values will soon cause us to question the fairness and justice of many of our past and present policies. . . . A true revolution of values will soon look uneasily on the glaring contrast of poverty and wealth.
—Martin Luther King Jr. (1929–1968)

A sleeping giant has awoken. After being told that there is nothing we can do to stop the greed, looting, and growing inequalities, the 99 percent now knows the world doesn't have to be this way.

The global 1 percent has recovered; their wealth is largely intact and they are back at the speculative gaming table. Meanwhile, the rest of the world is reeling from deep unemployment, anxious employment, diminished wealth, and insecurity.[1]

The Year of the Protester

In January 2012, *Time* magazine named the protester as its Person of the Year. All around us are signs of emerging social movements, pointing the way toward a new economy. After seeing their dreams shattered, the 99 percent got organized.

Now the streets are filled with chants and signs: WALL STREET GOT BAILED OUT, WE GOT FORECLOSED. Vast numbers of Americans identify with the rallying cry "We are the 99 percent."

Emerging Movements of the Global 99 Percent

The most visible U.S. movement in the fall of 2011 was the Occupy movement. But there have been many other mobilizations of people that contributed to the awakening. In the aftermath of the 2008 economic meltdown, a mammoth wave of discontent rumbled across the globe.

Arab Spring Protests. Across the Middle East, from Tunisia and Egypt to Syria and Pakistan, social movements are emerging to challenge tyranny and inequality of wealth and power. Led primarily by technologically networked youth, these movements have global interconnections and inspire one another.

Global Movement Against Corporate Tax Dodging. A global movement emerged in late 2010 to push back against corporations that dodge taxes and loot national treasuries. In the fall of 2010, U.K. activists organized direct action protests inside the storefronts of corporate tax dodgers. In February 2011, US Uncut was formed with creative actions in forty different cities. On April 15, 2011—tax day—there were more than 200 demonstrations at the local offices of corporate tax dodgers such as Bank of America, Verizon, Apple, and Federal Express.[2]

The 99 Percent in Wisconsin Get Organized. In February 2011, newly elected Wisconsin governor Scott Walker began to attack workers' rights and unions in Wisconsin, proposing legislation to abolish collective bargaining. He awoke workers and students, and a broad 99 percent coalition emerged to push back against his plans. This inspired movements in Ohio and other states to fight back against the phony austerity programs, budget cuts, and anti-worker agenda imposed by governors who cater to the 1 percent.

Tea Party Discontent. After the meltdown, the Tea Party movement emerged with a focus primarily on shrinking government.

While the infrastructure of organizations supporting the Tea Party was funded largely by people in the 1 percent, there is a grassroots base of people in the 99 percent who are furious at Wall Street and corporate excess. Leaders such as Ron Paul are challenging the role of the Federal Reserve in favoring the 1 percent at the expense of the 99 percent.

The Other 98 Percent. In April 2010, the Other 98 Percent emerged as a vibrant social media activist network. With more than 140,000 friends on Facebook, this group began to introduce the meme "We are the 98 percent," a year and a half before the Occupy Wall Street protests.

Public Outcry over Obama's Cave-In to the 1 Percent. In November 2010, President Obama cut a deal with Republican leaders to extend the Bush-era tax cuts for the 1 percent, after having campaigned to let them expire. The bottom 99 percent and allies in the 1 percent felt a tremendous sense of betrayal. Senator Bernie Sanders (I-Vt.) took to the Senate floor to deliver a historic eight-hour speech about the dangers of extreme inequality. The nation realized it couldn't wait for the president to lead on inequality issues; the 99 percent had to press for change.

Global Anti-Austerity Movements. Across the world, from Spain to Israel to India, people are taking to the streets to challenge austerity politics, which require budget cuts that hurt the 99 percent, and to protest tax and trade policies that favor the 1 percent. They are protesting the failure of their political systems, captured by the 1 percent, to address concerns about joblessness, affordable housing, and service and budget cuts.[3]

The American Dream Movement. An alliance of hundreds of organizations and millions of individuals have joined together concerned about the implosion of the middle-class standard of living. The American dream movement is working to rebuild the dream and build a power base to counter austerity policies that favor the 1 percent.[4]

Anti–Wall Street Protests and Move Your Money. Several co-alitions have come together to pressure Wall Street banks to stop home foreclosures and be more responsive to community needs. The move-your-money movement has inspired 650,000 people to close bank accounts at Wall Street banks that trashed the economy, relocating those billions in deposits to community banks and credit unions committed to meeting local credit needs.[5]

Nurses Organize to "Heal America and Tax Wall Street." National Nurses United has taken the lead in campaigning for a financial speculation tax as their prescription for "healing America" from Wall Street greed and excess. Tens of thousands of member nurses have marched on Wall Street and Congress. They have set up nursing stations at Occupy protest locations around the country.[6]

Circle of Protection. In the face of federal budget cuts, religious leaders from across the denominational and political spectrum have joined together to call on the Obama administration and Congress to draw a "circle of protection" around public programs that aid the poor. Christian members have asked, "What would Jesus cut?" challenging politicians who profess to be Christians to follow their religious teachings and protect the poor.[7]

Caring Across Generations. A powerful alliance of domestic workers, day laborers, and health care workers has joined together to campaign for higher standards of patient care and employment benefits for community health aides and caretakers, whose ranks will grow by 3 million in the next two decades.[8]

The 1 Percent in Support of the 99 Percent

Not just the 99 percent is waking up. The movement to build an economy that works for everyone is enlisting allies within the 1 percent.

The good news is there are people in the 1 percent who support the aspirations of the 99 percent. As mentioned earlier, the 1 percent is by no means a monolithic group. We've talked about the rule riggers, organized segments of the 1 percent that have teamed up with Wall Street leaders of the corporate 1 percent to use their power to preserve and expand their privileges. But not everyone in the 1 percent backs this program.

Polls indicate, for example, that over 65 percent of people in the 1 percent agree with the concerns of the 99 percent and believe they should pay more taxes. They recognize that the tax system is out of balance and that they've gotten generous tax breaks over the last decade.

The 1 Percent Gets Organized . . . for a Fairer Economy

The pro–99 percent segment of the 1 percent is getting organized and beginning to speak out. In 2010, a network called Wealth for the Common Good brought together business leaders and wealthy individuals concerned about inequality and supportive of fair tax policies. They launched a petition to encourage Congress to let the 2001 and 2003 Bush-era tax cuts expire. More than 500 people with incomes over $250,000—those who would pay the higher tax rates—publicly supported this call.

Wealth for the Common Good spearheaded an effort called Business and Investors Against Tax Haven Abuse. Linking up with coalitions representing more than 55,000 small businesses, including Business for Shared Prosperity and the Main Street Alliance, they lobbied to close the offshore system that enables companies and wealthy individuals to dodge billions in taxes. In 2010 and 2011, they convened several press conferences with Senator Carl Levin (D-Mich.), lead sponsor of the Stop Tax Haven Abuse legislation in Congress, to voice business support for the bill.[9]

In the fall of 2010, when President Obama cut a deal with Republican leaders to retain the tax cuts for the rich, there was a mini-rebellion among the members of the 1 percent who believe in the common good. Patriotic Millionaires for Fiscal Strength, a group of 250 millionaires, urged the president and Congress to "tax me."

In August 2011, Congress was engaged in a debate over whether to raise the debt ceiling. Conservatives in Congress argued that "raising revenue was off the table," that our deficit and debt problems could be solved only by cuts to spending. Warren Buffett published an op-ed in the *New York Times* called "Stop Coddling the Super-Rich" in which he disclosed that he pays a significantly smaller percentage of his income in taxes than his secretary and other co-workers. The reason for this is low capital gains rates. Buffett's income from investments is taxed at a 15 percent rate, whereas wage income is taxed at rates as high as 35 percent.

The Buffett statement and the growing understanding about corporate tax dodging touched a nerve. Many in the 99 percent viscerally understood they were being asked to make enormous sacrifices through budget cuts that would have consequences for millions of people. These cuts would affect already strapped schools, result in layoffs of firefighters and police officers, and reduce local aid, leading to closures of public facilities and the curtailment of youth programs. People in the 1 percent have family members who struggle with their mental health, and so they recognize that cuts in mental health services will overburden families who have a loved one with mental health challenges.

Media coverage and protests have dramatized how the top 1 percent is today paying a lower percentage of their income in taxes than has been the case for decades. And hundreds of corporations are paying no or extremely low taxes, thanks to aggressive tax dodging. Public opinion polls reflect that the 99 percent and the 1 percent didn't buy the we-are-broke austerity baloney.[10]

As the Occupy Wall Street movement moved into public squares around the country in September 2011 and people started to circulate photos and "We are the 99 percent" statements, some in the 1 percent were inspired. Elspeth Gilmore showed up at an Occupy Wall Street event with a sign that said,

> I inherited money at 21.
> I have had health and dental insurance all my life.
> I want to live in a world where we all have enough.
> I have more than enough.
> Tax me!
> I am the 1%.
> I stand with the 99%.[11]

A week later, a website was launched called 1 Percent Standing with the 99 Percent. Hundreds of people in the 1 percent started to send their photos and statements to the site.

Farhad Ebrahimi, who was active with Occupy Boston, wrote,

> I have an amount of money that is much more than I need. I AM THE 1%. My taxes are at a historical low, and the influence of money on our government is at a historical high. These are not good things! So what am I doing about it? (1) I am donating the vast majority of my money to social change organizations. (2) I am personally advocating for the repair of our broken system. I STAND WITH THE 99%. I am part of Occupy Boston. My money gives me no special influence here. That's the way it should be.

Motivations of the 1 Percent for the Common Good

Why are people in the 1 percent publicly stepping up and declaring their support for the bottom 99 percent? What are their motivations? In interviews I've conducted, people in the 1 percent express several reasons for supporting an economy that works for everyone.

Simple Fairness. Those among the 1 percent who care about the common good have witnessed the collapse of the middle-class standard of living and see how the budget cuts are hitting home. They comprehend the impact on their friends and neighbors in the 99 percent who lack decent health care and live with the stresses and insecurities of the current economy. The 1 percent travels the globe, so they sometimes have a firsthand picture of global inequalities and the fundamental unfairness of a system in which some are born to persistent poverty while others reap unending riches. While some in the 1 percent look at these inequalities and are content to wrap themselves in self-justifying explanations about why they deserve all their wealth, these myths are unraveling for the majority.

Long-Term Self-Interest in Reversing the Inequality Death Spiral. There are self-interested reasons the 1 percent might support greater equality. They understand that too much inequality has led to the inequality death spiral and greater economic instability, which in turn jeopardizes the wealth of the 1 percent. Some understand the dangers of an economy in which so many have so little and the consumer power of the former middle class has evaporated. The 1 percent has a front-row seat from which to watch the flow of wealth into speculative investments. They worry about rebellion and class war and understand that we don't want to become like Brazil, where wealthy elites hire bodyguards and must drive their bulletproof Mercedes-Benzes between their gated residential areas and shopping and dining enclaves for the super-rich.

Legacy for the Next Generation. Many in the 1 percent are parents and grandparents who are asking the question, "What kind of world are we leaving for the next generation?" While they personally might be content to live behind walls or on fortified islands of wealth, they know their children hunger to go forth into the world. Do they want them to live in an apartheid-like society? The fear of living in a grotesquely unequal society touches the 1 percent. But many are also moved by a sense of legacy, an understanding that they have a responsibility to leave the campsite cleaner than they found it, to pass on a society similar to the one that made their own opportunities possible.

No One Does It Alone. Many in the 1 percent know they did not get where they are entirely as a result of their own effort and hard work. They didn't do it alone. They understand the role of luck, inheritance, and the social and public investments that made their own good fortune possible.[12] Everyone in the United States, even those we might celebrate as having entirely bootstrapped themselves into wealth, inherited at birth a society that had unusual preconditions for enterprise development and wealth expansion.

The Greatest Generation, those who came of age during World War II, taxed themselves at very progressive levels in order to make investments in education, technological research, infrastructure, and middle-class expansion and opportunity that served as the foundation for the healthy and vibrant economy we enjoyed in the years after 1960.

Members of Patriotic Millionaires for Fiscal Strength and the Wealth for the Common Good network are very articulate—even poetic—in their statements about why they should pay more taxes. AOL co-founder Charlie Fink said, "You should tax me because our country is more important than my money."

9 Reversing the Inequality Death Spiral

The form of law which I propose would be as follows: In a state which is desirous of being saved from the greatest of all plagues—not faction, but rather distraction—there should exist among the citizens neither extreme poverty nor, again, excessive wealth, for both are productive of great evil. . . . Now the legislator should determine what is to be the limit of poverty or of wealth.
—Plato (c. 424–348 BCE)

How can we reverse the inequality death spiral that is wrecking the world? What must we do? What actions and policies will make the biggest difference?

A century ago, people reversed the excessive inequalities of the first Gilded Age. People learned the truth about the economy, got organized, built powerful social movements, and pressed for change. It took a generation, just as it took a generation for present-day inequalities to reach extreme levels.

Transition to a New Economy

This time around will be very different, as the world has changed. We must not only press for policies that reduce inequality but also make a nimble transition to a new economy based on an entirely different model of economic growth.

We're not going back to an economy based on excessive consumption of Earth's finite resources. We will not be able to return to an economy based on cheap, easy-to-get oil. Quite the opposite. The old paradigm of "priming the pump" with government spending to generate mass consumption will not be the path to an economy based on shared prosperity. We are stepping forward to a new economy, one based on an entirely different set of values, ecological limits, and aspirations.[1]

To succeed, we must shut down the Wall Street inequality machine and stop the reckless and shortsighted behavior of game fixers in the top 1 percent. We can't just tinker around the edges or try to merely contain their excesses.

Wall Street must be transformed. The speculators on Wall Street have added little value to the real economy in which the 99 percent live. Some in the 1 percent will try to convince us that without speculative Wall Street, we will be impoverished—we will destroy the goose that laid the golden egg. This is not true, and many of the 99 percent will be unmoved by these arguments.

We must deploy our creative energies and resources—including those of our allies in the 1 percent—and direct them toward building a new economy that operates within Earth's real limits and creates healthy livelihoods for all. We must build an economy that works for the 100 percent, not the 1 percent.

Across the world, the bottom 99 percent is organizing social movements for food security, access to water, fair trade, and the basic right to a decent life and livelihood. Those of us in the global North's industrialized countries—the wealthiest 5 percent—should ally ourselves with the 99 percent globally, support their struggles for sovereignty and economic independence, and not inadvertently side with the global rule fixers.

No single program for change will do the trick; we need a bundle of policies and practices that will reengineer the economy to share wealth and opportunity rather than funnel it to the 1 percent.

Changing rules alone, without changing our values and the colossal imbalance of power, will not succeed.

Extreme inequality has led to a downward spiral, as power concentrates further in the top 1 percent and a segment of them use their power to change the rules to shift further wealth toward themselves. One of our challenges is to identify the key ways to intervene in the spiral—the pressure points where we can direct our organized energy to reverse the downward momentum. Strategically identifying these pressure points will help us avoid wasting time on less effective strategies.

Three Shifts: Values, Power, and Rules

Three fundamental shifts that have fueled the downward inequality spiral have taken place. There has been a shift in *values* in our culture, the norms and stories that guide our way of thinking and living. There has been a shift in *power*, from the 99 percent to the 1 percent. And there has been a shift in the *rules* governing the economy, to benefit the 1 percent at the expense of the 99 percent. Each of these three shifts—values, power, and rules—interacts with and reinforces the others.

For example, as the values of our society shift to become more individualistic, we see some withdrawal of support from community institutions that uphold the common good. As wealth concentrates in fewer hands, some pursue a narrower, more selfish interest and use their wealth to lobby for policies that weaken community institutions and increase their own wealth.

In this chapter, we'll explore the shifts in values and power that have taken place and examine strategies that will help reverse inequality. We'll leave a discussion of the rule shifts that have affected the economy for the next chapter.

Figure 13. The inequality death spiral. As wealth concentrates in the hands of the 1 percent, they use their power to rig the rules to their benefit. This leads to a downward spiral in the quality of life for the bottom 99 percent.

Shifting Values

We won't be successful in building an economy that works for the 100 percent and the planet unless we shift our values. Extreme inequalities emerged because our society tolerated them—and even in some cases believed they were justified.

Dominant Values and Stories. The dominant values and social messages of the last three decades have included:

- You are on your own.
- Look out for #1.
- Consume without regard to the Earth or others.
- Do whatever you want, the sooner the better.
- Tough luck if you can't keep up.
- Everything will work out if we each pursue our individual self-interest.
- People are located along the economic ladder based on merit and deservedness.

Reversing inequality will require a shift away from some of these values, alongside changes in the distribution of power and the rules of the economy.

How do our beliefs and societal stories reinforce inequality? What are the pressure points in the area of values and stories? Reversing inequality will require us to elevate community-oriented values and address some of the cultural myths and stories that perpetuate inequality.

Community Values. To make a transition to the new economy, we need a new set of values and stories to guide us. These include the principles and recognition that:

- No one should be left behind; everyone has a gift to share.
- We should not organize people to serve the market; rather, the economy should be organized to support the flourishing of life, both human and natural.

Values and norms have shifted away from community values toward more individualist values—for example, the belief that "we're on our own."

Power has shifted from the 99 percent and Main Street businesses to the top 1 percent and several thousand multinational corporations. For example, campaign contributions of the top 1 percent trump the votes of the bottom 99 percent.

The rules and policies governing the economy have been changed. For example, increases in the minimum wage have been blocked at the same time as tax cuts have gone to the wealthy.

Figure 14. Since the late 1970s, we've lived through three shifts: a shift in values, a shift in power, and a shift in the rules governing the economy.

- We should adopt a seven-generation perspective—the belief that our actions should be considered in light of their impact seven generations into the future.
- No one does it alone. No one is an island. We are all recipients of help and investments made by previous generations. We have an obligation to pass on the gifts.
- We all do better when everyone does better.
- An injury to one is an injury to all.
- In religious traditions, we are one body.
- We can't ignore the downstream consequences of our actions.

These values are foundational and reflect the kind of society we are and will become.

Shifting Power

The gap between the 1 percent and the 99 percent is the result of a fundamental power shift within U.S. society. Main Street's small businesses have lost clout while Wall Street's corporations have increased their power in our democracy. The power of organized labor has declined while the power of corporate lobbyists has increased. The power of voters has been diminished by the 1 percent's money power flowing into the system. The power of organized civic groups has been displaced by the power of corporations and the capture of our political system (campaigns, elections, and lawmaking) by the corporate 1 percent.

At present, there is a political impasse. Public opinion and the 99 percent want our political leaders to put forward some very different priorities and changes, as discussed in chapter 4. The 99 percent wants increased oversight of Wall Street banks and reckless corporations. It wants millionaires to pay their fair share of taxes. It wants consumers to be protected from predatory elements of the credit card industry. Yet these changes are blocked by the 1 percent, which holds disproportionate power over our political system.

Pressure for positive change will keep building, however. The key will be when enough people in the 99 percent are organized to demand change and remove elected officials who are serving the 1 percent. For this to happen, a critical mass of the 99 percent will have to join organized efforts for change.

Building power today will look different than it did in the past, thanks to social media such as Facebook and Twitter. But it will also include face-to-face, people-to-people organizations and demonstrations, as in past generations. For this reason, drawing inspiration and strategic insights from social movements of the past is important. The rural Populist movement, with different tributaries from the 1880s to 1920s, organized for decades to press for changes that would reverse the inequalities and corruption of the first Gilded Age.[2]

There is presently a huge power imbalance between the top 1 percent and the 99 percent, between Wall Street and Main Street. Shifting this balance will require people to come together, form organizations, engage in civic life and politics, and lift up new values into our public life. It will require us to build powerful organizations to elect political representatives who serve the 100 percent, not just the 1 percent, and to hold them accountable. Several of these organizations were discussed in the previous chapter. Consider some of these forms of organization and how you might relate to them.

Worker Organizations. Unions, workers' centers, and workers' rights groups have been under attack for the last forty years. But post-Wisconsin, many are finding new energy to defend workers' rights and the middle-class standard of living. New formations of workers, such as Working America, knock on millions of doors a year. And the Fight for a Fair Economy campaign has animated activists in twenty major urban areas.

Faith-Rooted Organizing. Many religious congregations and people of faith have formed powerful local coalitions to bring their religious values into the public square. Networks such as PICO, Gamaliel, the Industrial Areas Foundation, and DART are building from the institutional rootedness of congregations and their depth of members to be a new force for social change.

New Civic-Organizing and "Net Roots" Campaigns. There's a new generation of "Net roots" organizing that includes networks such as MoveOn.org, Color of Change, and the Other 98 Percent. These networks aggregate power, money, and people for action. They also drive people to join emerging direct-action groups such as New Bottom Line, US Uncut, and the Occupy Wall Street mobilizations. Through these movements, people are finding neighbors, meeting up, and taking to the streets in support of change.

Affinity Groups and Local Support Circles. How do we break through isolation to get support when we lose our jobs or our homes or otherwise feel economic insecurity creeping up on us? How do we prepare to participate in nonviolent direct action and protests in our communities? How do we personally prepare for the transition to the new economy? Thousands of people in the United States are forming affinity groups, resilience circles, common-security clubs, and rebuilding-the-dream circles to provide mutual aid, share learning about the changing economy, and take social action with others. The small group cell is an important part of social movements going forward.

These groups are the building blocks of social movements. People don't act alone, nor do real, powerful campaigns emerge with only small groups of people working at the core. To succeed in advancing a program of rule changes, such as those we'll discuss in chapter 10, requires people power and organization.

10 Bold Rule Changes to Break Up Concentrated Wealth

In a world of increasing inequality, the legitimacy of institutions that give precedence to the property rights of "the Haves" over the human rights of "the Have Nots" is inevitably called into serious question.
—David Korten (1937)

We must change the rules of the economy so that they serve and lift up the 100 percent, not just the 1 percent. Starting in the mid-1970s, the rules were changed to reorient the economy toward the short-term interests of the 1 percent. We can shift and reverse the rules to work for everyone.

Three Types of Rule Changes

There are three categories of policy changes that we need: rules and policies that raise the floor, those that level the playing field, and those that break up overconcentrations of wealth and corporate power. These are not hard-and-fast categories, but a useful framework for grouping different rule changes.

1. **Rule changes that raise the floor**
   - Ensure the minimum wage is a living wage
   - Provide universal health care
   - Enforce basic labor standards and protections

2. **Rule changes that level the playing field**
   - Invest in eduction
   - Reduce the influence of money in politics
   - Implement fair trade rules

3. **Rule changes that break up wealth and power**
   - Tax the 1 percent
   - Rein in CEO pay
   - Stop corporate tax dodging
   - Reclaim our financial system
   - Reengineer the corporation
   - Redesign the tax revenue system

Figure 15. Three types of rule changes to reduce inequality.

Rule Changes That Raise the Floor

Policies that raise the floor reduce poverty and establish a fundamental minimum standard of decency that no one will fall below. The Nordic countries—Norway, Sweden, Denmark, and Finland—have very low levels of inequality, and they are also societies with strong social safety nets and policies that raise the floor.

One-third of people in the United States have no paid sick days, and one-half have no paid vacation days. Everyone deserves the right to take time off when sick and have a few weeks of vacation each year. In the rest of the developed world, these are considered basic human rights.

Examples of rule changes include:

Ensure the Minimum Wage Is a Living Wage. The minimum wage has lagged behind rising basic living expenses in housing, health care, transportation, and child care.

Provide Universal Health Care. Expand health coverage so that every child and adult has a minimum level of decent health care. No one should become sick or destitute because of lack of access to health care.

Enforce Basic Labor Standards and Protections. Ensuring basic worker rights and standards can lift up the bottom 20 percent of workers who are particularly exploited and disadvantaged in the current system. These rule changes include the forty-hour work-week, minimum vacation and family medical leave, sick leave, and protections against wage theft. Such rules contribute to a more humane society for everyone.

Rule Changes That Level the Playing Field

Policies and rule changes that level the playing field eliminate the unfair wealth and power advantages that flow to the 1 percent. Examples include:

Invest in Education. In the current global economy, disparities in education reinforce and contribute to inequality trends. Public investment in education is one of the most important interventions we can make to reduce inequality over time. "Widespread education has become the secret to growth," writes World Bank economist Branko Milanovic. "And broadly accessible education is difficult to achieve unless a society has a relatively even income distribution."[1]

Reduce the Influence of Money in Politics. Through various campaign finance reforms—including public financing of elections—we can reduce the nexus between gigantic wealth and political influence. Reforms include limits to campaign contributions, a ban on corporate contributions and influence, and a requirement for timely disclosure of donations.

Implement Fair Trade Rules. Most international free trade treaties have boosted the wealth of the 1 percent, whose members are the largest shareholders of global companies. Free trade rules often pit countries against one another in a race to lower standards addressing child labor, environmental protection, workers' rights to organize, and corporate regulation. Countries with the weakest standards are rewarded in this system. Fair trade rules would raise environmental and labor standards, so companies compete on the basis of other efficiencies.

Rule Changes That Break Up Wealth and Power

We can raise the floor and work toward a level playing field, but we cannot stop the perverse effects of extreme inequality without boldly advocating for policies that break up excessive concentrations of wealth and corporate power.

None of the raise-the-floor and level-the-playing-field rule changes and policy adjustments described above will succeed unless we directly tackle the great imbalance of wealth and power.

For example, we cannot pass campaign finance laws that seek clever ways to limit the influence of the 1 percent, as they will always find ways to subvert the law. Concentrated wealth is like water flowing downhill: it cannot stop itself from influencing the political system. The only way to fix the system is to not have such high levels of concentrated wealth. We need to level the hill!

This section examines several far-reaching policy initiatives, the tough changes that have to be considered if we're going to reverse extreme inequality. Some of these proposals have been off the public agenda for decades or have never been seriously considered.

Tax the 1 Percent. Historically, taxing the 1 percent is one of the most important rule changes that have reduced the concentration of wealth. In 1915, Congress passed laws instituting federal income taxes and inheritance taxes (estate taxes). Over the subsequent decades, these taxes helped reduce the concentrations of income and wealth and even encouraged Gilded Age mansions to be turned over to civic groups and charities.[2]

Taxes on higher income and wealth reached their zenith in the mid-1950s. At the time, the incomes of millionaires were taxed at rates over 91 percent. Today, the percentage of income paid by millionaires in taxes has plummeted to 21 percent. Back then, corporations contributed a third of the nation's revenue. Today, corporations pay less than one-tenth of the nation's revenue. The corporate 1 percent pays an average of 11.1 percent of income in taxes, down from 47.4 percent in 1961.[3]

Taxes on the wealthy have steadily declined over the last fifty years. If the 1 percent paid taxes at the same actual effective rate as they did in 1961, the U.S. Treasury would receive an additional $231 billion a year.[4] In 2009, the most recent year for which data are available, 1,500 millionaires paid no income taxes, largely because they dodged taxes through offshore tax schemes, according to the IRS.[5]

As with inequality, the higher up the income ladder people are, the lower the percentage of income they pay in taxes. This is why Warren Buffett's disclosure about his own low taxes was so important. Buffett revealed that in 2010, he paid only 14 percent of his income in federal taxes, lower than the 25 or 30 percent rate that his co-workers paid. Buffett wrote:

While the poor and middle class fight for us in Afghanistan, and while most Americans struggle to make ends meet, we mega-rich continue to get our extraordinary tax breaks. Some of us are investment managers who earn billions from our daily labors but are allowed to classify our income as "carried interest," thereby getting a bargain 15 percent tax rate. Others own stock index futures for 10 minutes and have 60 percent of their gain taxed at 15 percent, as if they'd been long-term investors.

These and other blessings are showered upon us by legislators in Washington who feel compelled to protect us, much as if we were spotted owls or some other endangered species. It's nice to have friends in high places.

The richest 400 taxpayers have seen their effective rate decline from over 40 percent in 1961 to 18.1 percent in 2010.[6]

Between 2001 and 2010, the United States borrowed almost $1 trillion to give tax breaks to the 1 percent. The 2001 and 2003 tax cuts passed under President George W. Bush were highly targeted to the top 1 and 2 percent of taxpayers. They included reducing the top income tax rate, cutting capital gains and dividend taxes, and eliminating the estate tax, our nation's only levy on inherited wealth.

Are we focusing too much on taxing millionaires, given the magnitude of our fiscal and inequality problems? Won't we have to raise taxes more broadly?[7] It is true that taxing the 1 percent won't entirely solve our nation's short-term deficit problems or dramatically reduce inequality in the short run. But it will have a meaningful impact on both problems over time. Thirty years of tax cuts for the 1 percent have shifted taxes onto middle-income taxpayers; they have also added to the national debt, which simply postpones additional tax increases on the middle class. Progressive taxes, as were seen in the United States after World War I and during the Great Depression, do chip away at inequalities. These extreme inequalities weren't built in a day, and the process of reversing them will not be instant, either. But when there is less concentrated income and wealth, there will be less money available for the 1 percent to use to undermine the political rule-making process.

Rein in CEO Pay. The CEOs of the corporate 1 percent are among the main drivers of the Wall Street inequality machine. They both push for rule changes to enrich the 1 percent and extract huge amounts of money for themselves in the process. But they are responding to a framework of rules that provide incentives to such short-term thinking. An early generation of CEOs operated within different rules and values—and they had a longer-term orientation.[8]

There is a wide range of policies and rule changes that could address the skewed incentive system that results in reckless corporate behavior and excessive executive pay. What follows are several principles and examples of reforms that will reduce concentrated wealth among the 1 percent and also reform corporate practices:

• *Encourage narrower CEO-worker pay gaps.* Extreme pay gaps— situations where top executives regularly take home hundreds of times more in compensation than average employees—run counter to basic principles of fairness. These gaps also endanger enterprise effectiveness. Management guru Peter Drucker, echoing the view of Gilded Age financier J. P. Morgan, believed that the ratio of pay between worker and executive could run no higher than twenty to one without damaging company morale and productivity.[9] Researchers have documented that Information Age enterprises operate more effectively when they tap into and reward the creative contributions of employees at *all* levels.[10]

An effective policy would mandate reporting on CEO-worker pay gaps. The 2010 Dodd-Frank financial reform legislation included a provision that would require companies to report the ratio between CEO pay and the median pay for the rest of their employees. This simple reporting provision is under attack, but should be defended, and the pay ratio should become a key benchmark for evaluating corporate performance.[11]

• *Eliminate taxpayer subsidies for excessive executive pay.* Ordinary taxpayers should not have to foot the bill for excessive executive compensation. And yet they do—through a variety of tax and accounting loopholes that encourage executive pay excess. These perverse incentives add up to more than $20 billion per year in forgone revenue.[12] One example: no meaningful regulations currently limit how much companies can deduct from their taxes for the expense of executive compensation. Therefore, the more firms pay their CEO, the more they can deduct off their federal taxes.

An effective policy would limit the deductibility of excessive compensation. The Income-Equity Act (HR 382) would deny all firms tax deductions on any executive pay that runs over twenty-five times the pay of the firm's lowest-paid employee or $500,000, whichever is higher. Companies can pay whatever they want, but over a certain amount, taxpayers shouldn't have to subsidize it. Such deductibility caps were applied to financial bailout recipient firms and will be applied to health insurance companies under the health care reform legislation.

• *Encourage reasonable limits on total compensation.* The greater the annual reward an executive can receive, the greater the temptation to make reckless executive decisions that generate short-term earnings at the expense of long-term corporate health. Outsized CEO paychecks have also become a major drain on corporate revenues, amounting, in one recent period, to nearly 10 percent of total corporate earnings.[13] Government can encourage more reasonable compensation levels without having to micromanage pay levels at individual firms.

An effective policy would raise top marginal tax rates. As discussed earlier, taxing high incomes at higher rates might be the most effective way to deflate bloated pay levels. In the 1950s and 1960s, compensation stayed within more reasonable bounds, in part because of the progressive tax system.

- *Force accountability to shareholders.* On paper, the corporate boards that determine executive pay levels must answer to shareholders. In practice, shareholders have had virtually no say in corporate executive pay decisions. Recent reforms have made some progress toward forcing corporate boards to defend before shareholders the rewards they extend to corporate officials.

An effective policy would give shareholders a binding voice on compensation packages. The Dodd-Frank reform includes a provision for a nonbinding resolution on compensation and retirement packages.

- *Accountability to broader stakeholders.* Executive pay practices, we have learned from the run-up to the 2008 financial crisis, impact far more than just shareholders. Effective pay reforms need to encourage management decisions that take into account the interests of all corporate stakeholders, not just shareholders but also consumers, employees, and the communities where corporations operate.

An effective policy would ensure wider disclosure by government contractors. If a company is doing business with the government, it should be held to a higher standard of disclosure. Taxpayers, workers, and consumers should know the extent to which our tax dollars subsidize top management pay. One policy change would be to pass the Patriot Corporations Act to extend tax incentives and federal contracting preferences to companies that meet good-behavior benchmarks that include not compensating any executive at more than 100 times the income of the company's lowest-paid worker.[14]

Stop Corporate Tax Dodging. There are hundreds of large transnational corporations that pay no or very low corporate income taxes. These include Verizon, General Electric, Boeing, and Amazon. A common gimmick of the corporate 1 percent is to shift profits to subsidiaries in low-tax or no-tax countries such as the Cayman Islands. They pretend corporate profits pile up offshore while their losses accrue in the United States, reducing or eliminating their company's obligation to Uncle Sam.

These same companies, however, use our public infrastructure—they hire workers trained in our schools, they depend on the U.S. court system to protect their property, and our military defends their assets around the world—yet they're not paying their share of the bill. In a time of war, the unequal sacrifice and tax shenanigans of these companies are even more unseemly.

Corporate tax dodging hurts Main Street businesses, the 99 percent that are forced to compete on a playing field that isn't level. "Small businesses are the lifeblood of local economies," said Frank Knapp, CEO of the South Carolina Small Business Chamber of Commerce. "We pay our fair share of taxes and generate most of the new jobs. Why should we be subsidizing U.S. transnationals that use offshore tax havens to avoid paying taxes?"[15]

This same offshore system facilitates criminal activity, from the laundering of drug money to the financing of terrorist networks. Smugglers, drug cartels, and even terrorist networks such as al-Qaeda thrive in secret offshore jurisdictions where individuals can hide or obscure the ownership of bank accounts and corporations to avoid any reporting or government oversight.[16]

The offshore system has spawned a massive tax-dodging industry. Teams of tax lawyers and accountants add nothing to the efficiency of markets or products. Instead of making a better widget, companies invest in designing a better tax scam. Reports about General Electric's storied tax dodging dramatize how modern transnationals view their tax accounting departments as profit centers.[17]

The combination of federal budget concerns and a growing public awareness of corporate tax avoidance will lead to greater focus on legislative solutions. One strategic rule change would be for Congress to pass the Stop Tax Haven Abuse Act, which would end costly tax games that are harmful to domestic U.S. businesses and workers and blatantly unfair to those who pay their fair share of taxes.

One provision of the act would treat foreign subsidiaries of U.S. corporations whose management and control are primarily in the United States as U.S. domestic corporations for income tax purposes. Another provision would require country-by-country reporting so that transnational corporations would have to disclose tax payments in all jurisdictions and not easily be able to pit countries against one another.[18]

The act would generate an estimated $100 billion in revenues a year, or $1 trillion over the next decade.

Reclaim Our Financial System. Wall Street and the top 1 percent have conducted a dangerous experiment on our lives. They have destroyed the livelihoods of billions of people around the planet in a bid to control the financial flows of the world and funnel money to the global 1 percent.

We sometimes forget that our financial sector is a human-created system that should serve the public interest and be subordinate to the credit needs of the real economy. Instead, we have a system where the planet is ruled by a tiny 1 percent of financial capital.

As quoted earlier, David Korten writes in "How to Liberate America from Wall Street Rule" that the "priority of the money system shifted from funding real investment for building community wealth to funding financial games designed solely to enrich Wall Street without the burden of producing anything of value."[19]

Communities across the country, as discussed earlier, are shifting funds out of the speculative banking sector and into community banks and lending institutions that are constructive lenders in the real economy.

More than 650,000 individuals have closed accounts at institutions such as Bank of America and moved their money. A number of religious congregations, unions, and civic organizations have followed suit. Now local governments are beginning to shift their funds. In the City of Boston, the City Council has voted to link deposits of public funds to institutions with strong commitments to community investments.[20]

Here are some interventions to break Wall Street's hold on our banking and money system.[21]

- *Break up the big banks.* Reverse the thirty-year process of banking concentration and support a system of decentralized, community-accountable financial institutions committed to meeting the real credit needs of local communities. Limit the size of financial institutions to several billion dollars, and eliminate government preferences and subsidies to Wall Street's too-big-to-fail banks in favor of the 15,000 community banks and credit unions that are already serving local markets.
- *Create a network of state-level banks.* Each state should have a partnership bank, similar to what's been in place in North Dakota since 1919. These banks would hold government funds and

private deposits and partner with community-based banks and other financial institutions to provide credit to enterprises and projects that contribute to the health of the local economy. The North Dakota experience has shown how a state bank can provide stability and curb speculative trends. North Dakota has more local banks than any other state and the lowest bank default rate in the nation.

- *Create a national infrastructure and reconstruction bank.* Instead of channeling Federal Reserve funds into private Wall Street banks, Congress should establish a federal bank to invest in public infrastructure and partner with other financial institutions to invest in reconstruction projects. The focus should be on investments that help make a transition to a green, sustainable economy.
- *Provide rigorous oversight of the financial sector.* The 2010 reforms to the financial sector failed to curtail some of the most destructive, gambling-oriented practices in the economy. The shadow banking system—including unregulated hedge funds—should be brought under greater oversight, like other utilities, and Congress should levy a financial speculation tax on transactions to pay for the oversight system.
- *Restructure the federal reserve.* The Federal Reserve has been creating money and channeling it to beneficiaries within the economy with no public accountability. The Fed contributed to the economic meltdown by failing to provide proper oversight for financial institutions under its jurisdiction, keeping easy credit flowing during an asset bubble, ignoring community banks, and then propping up bad financial actors. The Fed must be reorganized to be an independent federal agency with proper oversight and accountability. Its regulatory functions should be separated from its central bank functions, the new regulator given teeth to enforce rules, and individuals who work for the regulatory agency prevented from subsequently going to work for banks.

Reengineer the Corporation. The concentration of power in the corporate 1 percent has endangered our economy, our democracy, and the health of our planet. There is no alternative but to end corporate rule. This will require not only reining in and regulating the excesses of the corporate 1 percent but also rewiring the corporation as we know it.

Unfortunately, the Supreme Court's *Citizens United* (2010) decision moves things in the wrong direction, giving corporations greater "free speech" rights to use their wealth and power to change the rules of the economy. An essential first step in shifting the balance back to the 99 percent is reversing the *Citizens United* decision through congressional action.

There are good and ethical human beings working in corporations and in the 1 percent. But the hardwiring of these companies is toward the maximization of profits for absentee shareholders and toward reducing and shifting the cost of employees, taxes, and environmental rules that shrink profits. The current design of large global corporations enables them to dodge responsibilities and obligations to stakeholders, including employees, localities, and the ecological commons. The corporate 1 percent may pledge loyalty to the rule of law, but they spend an inordinate amount of resources lobbying to reshape or circumvent these laws, often by moving operations to other countries and to secrecy jurisdictions.

At the root of the problem is a power imbalance. Concentrated corporate power is unaccountable—and there is little countervailing force in the form of government oversight or organized consumer power.

Looking at corporate scandals such as those of Enron and AIG, or at the roots of the 2008 economic meltdown, we find case studies of the rule riggers within the corporate 1 percent using political clout to rewrite government rules, dilute accounting standards, intimidate or co-opt government regulators, or outright lie, cheat, and steal.

Changing the rules for the corporate 1 percent is not anti-business and, by creating a level playing field and a framework of fair rules, will actually strengthen the 99 percent of businesses that most contribute to our healthy economy. A new alignment of business organizations reflects this. The American Sustainable Business Council is an alternative to the U.S. Chamber of Commerce and advocates for high-road policies that will build a durable economy with broad prosperity.[22]

Communities have used a wide range of strategies to assert rights and power in relation to corporations. In 2007, the Strategic Corporate Initiative published an overview of these strategies in a report called "Toward a Global Citizens Movement to Bring Corporations Back Under Control." Many strategies are incremental, but worth understanding as part of the lay of the land in rule changes.[23]

- *Engage in consumer action.* As stakeholders, consumers have leverage to change corporate behavior. Examples include consumer boycotts that changed Nestlé's unethical infant formula marketing campaigns around the world and softened the hardball anti-worker tactics of companies such as textile giant J. P. Stevens. New technologies are enabling consumers to be more sophisticated in leveraging their power to force companies to treat employees and the environment better.[24]
- *Promote socially responsible investing.* Shareholders can also exercise power by avoiding investments in socially injurious corporations. In 2010, over $3 trillion in investments were managed with ethical criteria.[25] Companies do change some behaviors when concerned about their reputations.
- *Use shareholder power for the common good.* For more than forty years, socially concerned religious and secular organizations have utilized the shareholder process to change corporate behavior and management practices. Shareholder resolutions, in conjunc-

tion with educational and consumer campaigns, have altered corporate behavior, such as the movement to pressure U.S. companies to stop doing business in South Africa during the apartheid era.

- *Change rules inside corporations to foster accountability.* There are internal changes in corporate governance that potentially could broaden accountability and corporate responsibility. These include:
  - *Shareholder power reforms.* Presently, there are many barriers to the exercise of real shareholder ownership power and oversight. Corporations should have real governance elections, not hand-picked slates that rubber-stamp management decisions.
  - *Board independence.* Public corporations should have independent boards free of cozy insider connections. This will enable them to hold management properly accountable.
  - *Community rights.* Communities should have greater power to require corporate disclosure about taxes, subsidies, treatment of workers, and environmental practices, including use of toxic chemicals.
- *Require federal corporate charters.* Most U.S. corporations are chartered at the state level, and a number of states, including Delaware, have such low accountability requirements that they are home to thousands of global companies. But corporations above a certain size that operate across state and international boundaries should be subject to a federal charter.
- *Define stakeholder governance.* A federal charter could define the governing board of a corporation to include representation of all major stakeholders, including consumers, employees, localities where the company operates, and organizations representing environmental interests. The German experience with co-determination includes boards with community and employee representation.

- *Ban corporate influence in our democracy.* Corporations should be prohibited from any participation in our democratic systems, including elections, funding of candidates, political parties, party conventions, and advertising aimed at influencing the outcome of elections and legislation. This would require legislation to reverse the impact of the Supreme Court's *Citizens United* decision.

Citizens United and Corporate Power

In January 2010, the U.S. Supreme Court decided the case known as *Citizens United v. Federal Election Commission.* It gave new rights of free speech to corporations by saying that governments could not restrict independent spending by corporations and unions for political purposes. This opened the door for new election-related campaign spending and has given birth to super PACs that further erode the power of the 99 percent to influence national politics.

Senator Charles Schumer (D-N.Y.) sponsored legislation called the DISCLOSE Act to force better disclosure of campaign financiers, but it has been opposed by the U.S. Chamber of Commerce and other big business lobbies.

Other potential remedies include a push for an amendment to the Constitution to remove the free speech rights for corporations that *Citizens United* provides. Move to Amend is a coalition organizing such an amendment.

The reengineered corporation will still employ thousands of people and be innovative and productive. But it will be much more accountable to shareholders, to the communities in which it operates, and to customers, employees, and the common good.

Redesign the Tax Revenue System. This final section of rule changes examines how farsighted tax and revenue policies can aid in the transition to a new and sustainable economy. Present tax rules do not reflect the widely held values and priorities of the 99 percent. Rather, they reflect the designs and worldview of the powerful 1 percent of global corporations and wealthy individuals. The 1 percent devotes considerable lobbying clout to shaping and distorting our tax laws, which is one of the reasons those laws are so complex and porous.

Our tax revenue system should be simple, treat all fairly, and raise adequate revenue for the services we need. Tax rules and budgets are moral documents; we should not pretend they are value neutral.

We've already discussed two ways that the tax code has been distorted. The first is how it privileges income from wealth over income from work by taxing capital gains at absurdly low rates.[26] Second, the offshore system gives advantages to the global tax dodgers in the corporate 1 percent who force domestic businesses in the 99 percent to compete on an uneven playing field.

Another example is the way our tax code offers larger incentives to mature extractive industries such as oil and natural gas instead of directing resources to communities and corporations that conserve resources, care for the Earth, and catalyze new green enterprises.

The present tax system not only fails to raise adequate revenue from those most capable of paying but also serves as a huge impediment to progress. Current tax rules lock us into the economy of the past, rather than encouraging a transition to a new economy rooted in ecological sustainability, good jobs, and greater equality.

Conventional tax wisdom asserts that we should "tax the bads" by placing a higher price on harmful activities. Hence the notion of "sin taxes" levied on liquor, tobacco, and now, with increasing ferocity, junk food. Taxing these items raises revenue to offset the societal costs of alcoholism, cancer, and obesity. But sin taxes, like any sales tax, are regressive, requiring lower-income households to pay a higher percentage of their income than the wealthy pay.

There are three major "bads" that our tax code should be revised to address:

1. Extreme concentrations of income, wealth, and power that undermine social cohesion and a healthy democracy
2. Financial speculation, such as the activities that destabilized our economy in 2008
3. Pollution and profligate consumption that deplete our ecosystems

There are several bold interventions that focus on "taxing the bads" of our contemporary era and reversing two generations of tax shifts away from the 1 percent. They cluster around three foci: taxing concentrated wealth, taxing financial speculation, and taxing the destruction of nature.

- *Tax inheritances.* Levy a progressive estate tax on the fortunes of the 1 percent. At the end of 2010, Congress reinstated the estate tax on estates over $5 million ($10 million for a couple) at a 35 percent rate. Congress could close loopholes and raise additional revenue from the 1 percent with the greatest capacity to pay. The Responsible Estate Tax Act establishes graduated tax rates, with no tax on estates worth under $3.5 million, or $7 million for a couple, and includes a 10 percent surtax on the value of an estate above $500 million, or $1 billion for a couple. Estimated annual revenue: $35 billion.[27]
- *Institute a wealth tax on the 1 percent.* A "net worth tax" should be levied on individual or household assets, including real estate, cash, investment funds, savings in insurance and pension plans, and personal trusts. The law can be structured to tax wealth only above a certain threshold. For example, France's solidarity tax on wealth is for those who have assets in excess of $1.1 million.

- *Establish new tax brackets for the 1 percent.* Under our current tax rate structure, households with incomes over $350,000 pay the same top income tax rate as households with incomes over $10 million. In the 1950s, there were sixteen additional tax rates over the highest rate (35 percent) that we have today. A 50 percent rate on incomes over $2 million would generate an additional $60 billion a year.
- *Eliminate the cap on social security withholding taxes.* Extend the payroll tax to cover all wages, not just wage income up to $110,100. Today, some in the 1 percent are done paying their withholding taxes in January, while people in the 99 percent pay all year.
- *Institute a financial speculation tax.* A tax on financial transactions could generate significant funds for reinvesting in the transition to a financial system that works for everyone. Speculative trading now accounts for up to 70 percent of the trades in some markets. Commodity speculation unnecessarily bids up the cost of food, gasoline, and other basic necessities for the 99 percent. A modest federal tax on every transaction that involves the buying and selling of stocks and other financial products would both generate substantial revenue and dampen reckless risk taking. For ordinary investors, the cost would be negligible, like a tiny insurance fee to protect against financial instability. Estimated revenue: $150 billion a year.[28]
- *Tax income from wealth at higher rates.* Giving tax advantages to income from wealth also encourages speculation. As described by Warren Buffett and others, we can end this preferential treatment for capital gains and dividends and at the same time encourage average families to engage in long-term investing. Estimated revenue: $88 billion per year.
- *Tax carbon.* Instead of taxpayers paying indirectly for the expensive social costs associated with climate change, taxes could build some of these real costs into purchases and products. Perhaps the

most critical tax intervention to slow climate change would be to put a price on dumping carbon into the atmosphere from the transportation, energy, and other sectors. For example, the real ecological and societal costs of private jet travel would greatly increase the cost of owning or using private jets.[29] A gradually phased-in tax on carbon would create tremendous incentives to invest in energy conservation and regional green infrastructure. Proposals include a straight carbon tax or a cap-and-dividend proposal that would rebate 50 percent of revenue to consumers to offset the increased costs of some products and still generate $75–100 billion per year.[30] We could also explore similar taxes on other pollutants, such as nitrates that are destroying our water supplies.

- *Tax excessive consumption.* Consumption of unnecessary stuff, especially by the 1 percent, is filling our landfills and destroying our environment. A tax on certain nonessential goods, such as expensive jewelry and technological gadgets, would reflect the real ecological cost of such items. It could apply only to purchases that exceed a certain amount, such as cars that cost more than $100,000. Some states currently charge a luxury tax on high-end real estate transactions.

Objections by some in the 1 percent to these proposals will be strong, along with howls of "class warfare" and "job killing." Some will argue that government shouldn't be in the business of picking winners in the economy. But the reality is that our current tax policy is picking winners every day, and they're usually in the 1 percent.

For several generations after the introduction of a federal income tax at the end of the nineteenth century, our progressive federal tax system was moderately effective in reducing concentrations of wealth. As we briefly described, during the 1950s wealthy individuals paid significantly more taxes than they do today. Since 1980, however, we've lived through a great tax shift as lawmakers moved tax obligations off the wealthy and onto low- and middle-income taxpayers, off corporations and onto individuals, and off today's taxpayers and onto our children and grandchildren.

This program would reverse these tax shifts and set up signposts to help with the transition to the new economy.

CONCLUSION

Prospects for
Greater Equality

Photo © Ellen Shub.

If you have reached this point in the book (or jumped ahead), you probably have one central question on your mind: have we gone too far into the inequality death spiral to reverse direction?

After all, the more one stares into the abyss and comprehends the enormous social and ecological costs of extreme inequality, the more frightening the picture becomes. And assessing the power and resources available to the rule riggers is equally daunting. It appears that the top 1 percent and a few thousand corporations have a lock on our political system.

There is also, if we truly tune in, a great deal of brokenness around us—broken people, broken institutions, and broken trust. Extreme inequalities have shattered our communities and our psyches.

I don't want to be coy in my own assessment. I think things could go very badly. We are on a cusp of a huge transition in the life of our planet, with all kinds of change on the horizon. In the coming months and years, we are going to hit a number of economic and ecological shock points. These include further economic downturns, extreme weather events, disruptions to the food system, and other disorders that could lead to societal breakdown.

Heading into this transition with present levels of extreme inequality is dangerous for several reasons. First, the 1 percent holds disproportionate power and wealth, including much of the resources we need to fix our collective problems. Second, they have the power to confuse, delay, and even block the processes required to build resilient communities and implement longer-term policy changes.

Many in the 1 percent have little stake, at least in the short term, in participating in society-wide solutions. Their default position, in the face of fear and change, will be to withdraw to privileged fortresses and distance themselves from the worst side effects of the economic and ecological transition. Their distance is illusory, of course. The 1 percent cannot truly be buffered from the great transition we are about to live through. But their engagement may be delayed.

I'm very concerned, for example, that by the time the 1 percent wake up to the ecological climate crisis, we will have lost a huge amount of the advance time required to respond without serious disruptions.

That is my bleak view. But there are several signs of the times that give me tremendous hope and inspiration.

The Global Awakening of Social Movements. As *Time* magazine observed, 2011 was the year of the protester. Across the planet, people are taking to the streets, finding their voices and power. I anticipate an "American Spring"—an awakening in the coming years that will be unparalleled by anything we have seen in decades. The fundamental conditions of inequality, economic instability, and ecological precariousness will not change—and this will engage people.

Most encouraging is that people are not waiting for leaders to fix things. Most of the global movements of the 99 percent understand that the old political systems, and the elite 1 percent that dominates them, will not be able to solve these problems. We are heading into a time of tremendous transformation.

Allies in the 1 Percent. As I've documented in this book, there are tremendous allies within the top 1 percent who are also waking up and recognizing that the current drift is not in their fundamental interest. The 99 percent movement will have to figure out how to relate to these allies. But my view is that personal and strategic appeals to people in the 1 percent will be powerful and effective. We must invite the 1 percent to leave their illusory fortresses and enclaves of privilege and rejoin humanity, encouraging them to meet their needs through community and not through privatized paradises.

The Leaders Are Starting to Follow—but We're Not Waiting. In December 2011, President Obama gave a remarkable speech about inequality in the United States. He delivered these remarks in Osawatomie, Kansas—more than a century after former president Theodore Roosevelt gave a similar speech in the same city. Obama said that the financial crisis

> combined the breathtaking greed of a few with irresponsibility all across the system. And it plunged our economy and the world into a crisis from which we're still fighting to recover. It claimed the jobs and the homes and the basic security of millions of people— innocent, hardworking Americans who had met their responsibilities but were still left holding the bag.[1]

President Obama is attempting to get out ahead of public opinion. He is not leading so much as mirroring the shift in public consciousness about inequality. Other political leaders will be also running to the front of the parade, in a demonstration that the emerging social movements are changing our politics and our conversations about the economy. Regardless of the outcome of any particular future elections, this trend will continue. Politicians will bend to be understood as the "candidates of the 99 percent," and they will be judged by that measure.

We cannot wait for President Obama or anyone else to lead on these issues. Like each of us, President Obama, or whoever emerges as a future elected leader, is waiting to be called to something greater. Our job is to find the pressure points that open up the political system to rule changes that ensure we can build an economy that works for everyone, not just the 1 percent.

So this brings us back to the question of timing. Do we have time? In this book, I've argued that reversing the inequality death spiral is not a small job. I've pointed out that it took a generation to reverse the extreme inequalities of the first Gilded Age after 1929. I've observed that it took a generation of shifts in values, power, and rules between the mid-1970s and the present to bring us to this current moment in the inequality death spiral.

This implies that change will take time—another generation, perhaps—to reverse these changes. But here's the rub: this time we don't have the luxury of that many years to reverse the current inequality spiral. We're losing ground every day.

So I think we have to change our sense of time and of what is possible in the short term.

I need to reveal one personal bias or belief that is rooted in my own spiritual practice. An important source of my optimism is our personal and societal capacity for transformation. Each of us has a tremendous internal ability to heal from brokenness, which will transform not just our own lives but also the direction of our communities. We have the wherewithal to step up and respond to crisis at a wartime mobilization level.

In fact, I think each of us is waiting to be awakened and called forth to something fundamentally greater. I think there are millions of people around the world who are essentially half awake, sleepwalking through their days. But like a dormant seed, waiting for the right conditions of moisture, we are waiting to be called forth.

We could be called forth by fear and scarcity to a hunker-down orientation. But there is just as much possibility that we will be called forth to share community responses, which in the end is the only way forward.

In October 2011, I joined several thousand nurses marching in Washington, D.C., in support of a financial speculation tax on Wall Street trading. These nurses had traveled from all over the United States to join a protest march and lobby day.

I met a nurse from a hospital in Taunton, Massachusetts, who had taken an overnight bus to join the demonstration. She wore a bright red T-shirt that said, IF YOU SAVE A LIFE, YOU'RE A HERO. IF YOU SAVE A HUNDRED LIVES, YOU'RE A NURSE.

She told me she was sickened by trying to heal her neighbors of illnesses and injuries brought about by financial greed in her community. "I'm just a nurse," she explained. "But I can't just sit by and watch the victims of inequality and greed and stay silent."

Along with thousands of other nurses, she held a sign with a simple message: HEAL AMERICA. TAX WALL STREET. A year prior to this demonstration, these nurses were not in the streets. Most of them had probably never heard of a financial speculation tax. Yet here they were, by the thousands, making their voices heard.

I wondered: what would it take to get a million people marching like these nurses?

So I'd like to end this book with a personal invitation to you to explore what it means to step up.

I invite you to put down this book and pause. Sit quietly and think about the coming years and what role you will play in the changes ahead. Think of one or two people with whom you could talk about the times ahead and make plans. These challenges may feel overwhelming. But you can start small and manageable, with one-on-one conversations.

Eventually, I encourage you to think of ten people you could invite into a conversation. Your conversations might take the form of an affinity group or a resilience circle. Whatever you call it, it is a circle of people who will sit with one another and talk truthfully about how together you can face the future. With these people you should share the realities of your economic lives and your hopes and fears.

If this group is right, you will figure out how to support one another to build personal and community resilience and what actions to take together to organize and build power. I hope that you will learn to trust your intuition individually and together.

In the end, our small groups and circles will be part of the foundation for change, acting on some of the ideas I've offered in this book.

With you anything is possible.

Notes

Introduction: We Are the 99 Percent

1. We Are the 99 Percent website, http://wearethe99percent.tumblr.com /post/12556818590/i-also-wanted-to-go-to-a-top-university-which-i (accessed January 3, 2012).

2. We Are the 99 Percent website, http://wearethe99percent.tumblr.com /post/12639892423/i-am-a-27-year-old-veteran-of-the-iraq-war-i (accessed January 3, 2012).

3. We Stand with the 99 Percent website, http://westandwiththe99percent .tumblr.com/post/11849022824/i-made-millions-studying-the-math-of -mortgages-and (accessed January 3, 2012).

4. Sylvia A. Allegretto, "The State of Working America's Wealth," Economic Policy Institute Briefing Paper #292, March 23, 2011.

5. Sam Pizzigati, "The New Forbes 400—and Their $1.5 Trillion," inequality.org, September 25, 2011, http://inequality.org/forbes-400-15 -trillion (accessed January 3, 2012).

6. Sarah Anderson, Chuck Collins, Scott Klinger, and Sam Pizzigati, "The Massive CEO Rewards for Tax Dodging," Institute for Policy Studies, September 2011, www.ips-dc.org/reports/executive_excess_2011_the _massive_ceo_rewards_for_tax_dodging (accessed January 3, 2012).

7. Congressional Budget Office, "Trends in the Distribution of Household Income Between 1979 and 2007," October 2011, www.cbo.gov/doc.cfm ?index=12485Name (accessed January 3, 2012).

8. Kathy Ruffing and James Homey, "Economic Downturn and Bush Policies Continue to Drive Large Projected Deficits," Center on Budget and

Policy Priorities, May 10, 2011, www.cbpp.org/cms/?fa=view&id=3490 (accessed January 3, 2012).

Chapter 1: Coming Apart at the Middle

1. Kevin Phillips, *Politics of Rich and Poor: Wealth and the American Electorate in the Reagan Aftermath* (New York: HarperCollins, 1991).
2. The best example was Michael W. Cox and Richard Alm, *Myths of Rich and Poor: Why We're Better Off than We Think* (New York: Basic Books, 2000).
3. Alan Greenspan, "Income Inequality: Issues and Policy Options," at a symposium sponsored by the Federal Reserve Bank of Kansas City, Jackson Hole, Wyoming, August 28, 1998, www.federalreserve.gov/boarddocs /Speeches/1998/19980828.htm (accessed January 3, 2012).
4. Karlyn H. Bowman, "Public Attitudes About Economic Inequality," presentation at the American Enterprise Institute, May 20, 1997, www.aei .org/events/1997/05/20/public-attitudes-about-economic-inequality (accessed January 3, 2012).
5. Ibid. For attitudes in the UK, see Michael Orton and Karen Rowling-son, "Public Attitudes to Economic Inequality," Joseph Roundtree Founda-tion, July 2007, www.jrf.org.uk/sites/files/jrf/2097.pdf (accessed January 3, 2012).
6. Democracy Corps and Think Progress, "Economic Messages That Work—Lessons from Occupy Wall Street," October 25, 2011, www .americanprogressaction.org/issues/2011/10/pdf/economic_messages_that _work.pdf (accessed January 3, 2012).
7. Jeff Zeleny and Megah Thee-Brenan, "New Poll Finds a Deep Distrust of Government," *New York Times*, October 25, 2011, www.nytimes.com /2011/10/26/us/politics/poll-finds-anxiety-on-the-economy-fuels-volatility-in -the-2012-race.html. (accessed January 3, 2012).
8. We Are the 99 Percent website, http://wearethe99percent.tumblr.com (accessed January 3, 2012).
9. We Are the 99 Percent website, http://wearethe99percent.tumblr.com /post/12720481090/i-am-one-of-the-lucky-ones-i-fought-for-my (accessed January 3, 2012).
10. Kevin Phillips, *Wealth and Democracy: A Political History of the American Rich* (New York: Broadway Books, 2003), 68.
11. James L. Huston, *Securing the Fruits of Labor: The American Concept of Wealth Distribution, 1765–1900* (Baton Rouge: University of Louisiana

Press, 1998), 349. Also see Harold C. Livesay, *Andrew Carnegie and the Rise of Big Business* (Boston: Addison-Wesley, 1975); Ron Chernow, *The House of Morgan* (New York: Simon and Schuster, 1990); and Ron Chernow, *Titan: The Life of John D. Rockefeller Sr.* (New York: Random House, 1998).

12. Huston, *Securing the Fruits of Labor*, xviii.

13. Bill Gates Sr. and I discuss this in *Wealth and Our Commonwealth: Why American Should Tax Accumulated Fortunes* (Boston: Beacon Press, 2003).

14. The large trusts gave cash directly to candidates and politicians with the intention of buying their votes. It is widely accepted that corporate trusts, led by fund-raising master Mark Hanna, directly purchased the 1896 presidency of William McKinley, who ably served the political agenda of the corporate trusts. See Matthew Josephson, *The Robber Barons* (San Diego: Harcourt, Brace, 1934); and Edmund Morris, *Theodore Rex* (New York: Random House, 2001). Among the exposés were Ida Tarbell's pieces on Standard Oil that appeared in *McClure's* magazine in the 1890s and Lincoln Steffens' series "Shame of the Cities," chronicling bribery, machine politics, and corruption, also appearing in *McClure's*. See Phillips, *Wealth and Democracy*.

15. See Jeff Gates, *Democracy at Risk: Rescuing Main Street from Wall Street* (Cambridge, MA: Perseus Press, 2000), xii.

16. This history can best be found in Sam Pizzigati, *Greed and Good: Understanding and Overcoming the Inequality That Limits Our Lives* (New York: Apex Press, 2004).

17. For a history of the tax changes of the time, see Sidney Ratner, *Taxation and Democracy in America*, rev. ed. (New York: Wiley, 1967).

18. Phillips, *Wealth and Democracy*, 79. Also see the Economic Policy Institute's terrific interactive chart for the period 1917–2008: www.stateof workingamerica.org/pages/interactive#/?start=1917&end=1918, (accessed January 3, 2012).

19. See Paul Krugman, *The Conscience of a Liberal*, September 18, 2007, http://krugman.blogs.nytimes.com/2007/09/18/introducing-this-blog (accessed January 3, 2012).

20. Kenneth Jackson, *Crabgrass Frontier: The Suburbanization of the United States* (New York: Oxford University Press, 1985), 190–209.

21. Juliet B. Schor, *Born to Buy* (New York: Scribner, 2004), 10. Also see Larry Mishel, Jared Bernstein, and Sylvia Allegretto, "Fact Sheet on Work Hours," in *State of Working America, 2006–2007* (Washington, DC: Economy Policy Institute, 2006).

22. James Lardner et al., *Up to Our Eyeballs: The Hidden Truths and Consequences of Debt in Today's America* (New York: New Press, 2008).

Chapter 2: Who Is the 1 Percent?

1. Sylvia A. Allegretto, "The State of Working America's Wealth," Economic Policy Institute, Briefing Paper #292, March 23, 2011.

2. Congressional Budget Office, "Trends in the Distribution of Household Income Between 1979 and 2007," October 2011, www.cbo.gov /doc.cfm?index=12485Name (accessed January 3, 2012).

3. Lawrence Mishel and Josh Bivens, "Occupy Wall Streeters Are Right About Skewed Economic Rewards in the United States," Economic Policy Institute, Briefing Paper #331, October 26, 2011, www.epi.org/files/2011 /BriefingPaper331.pdf (accessed January 3, 2012).

4. Allegretto, "The State of Working America's Wealth," 10–14.

5. Ibid.

6. Larry Mishel, "Huge Disparity in Share of Total Wealth Gain Since 1983," Economic Policy Institute, September 15, 2011, www.epi.org /publication/large-disparity-share-total-wealth-gain (accessed January 3, 2012).

7. Robert Frank, *Richistan: A Journey Through the American Wealth Book and the Lives of the New Rich* (New York: Crown, 2007), 6–12.

8. See Thomas J. Stanley and William D. Danko, *Millionaire Next Door: The Surprising Secrets of America's Wealthy* (New York: Pocket Books, 1996).

9. Frank, *Richistan*, 11.

10. Mishel, "Huge Disparity."

11. Mishel and Bivens, "Occupy Wall Streeters Are Right"; and Mishel, "Huge Disparity."

12. Sam Pizzigati, "The New Forbes 400—and Their $1.5 Trillion," inequality.org, September 25, 2011, http://inequality.org/forbes-400-15 -trillion (accessed January 3, 2012).

13. Ibid.

14. Preliminary unpublished analysis by Chuck Collins, Peter Dreier, and Andrea Gordillo, based on Forbes 400 Wealth Report, October 2011.

15. Chuck Collins, Sam Pizzigati, and Alison Golberg, "Unnecessary Austerity," Institute for Policy Studies, April 2011, www.ips-dc.org/reports /unnecessary_austerity_unnecessary_government_shutdown (accessed January 3, 2012).

16. Merrill Lynch Global Wealth Management and Capgemini, "15th Annual World Wealth Report," June 22, 2011, www.capgemini.com/news -and-events/news/merrill-lynch-global-wealth-management-and-capgemini -release-15th-annual-world-wealth-report (accessed January 3, 2012).

17. Wealth-X, "World Ultra Wealth Report 2011," November 10, 2011, www.wealthx.com/articles/2011/wealth-x-launches-the-first-world-ultra -wealth-report (accessed January 3, 2012).

18. Credit Suisse, "Global Wealth Report," October 8, 2010, https://www
.credit-suisse.com/news/en/media_release.jsp?ns=41610 (accessed January 3,
2012).

Chapter 3: How the 1 Percent Rigs the Rules of the Economy

1. Luisa Kroll, "The Forbes 400: How Do America's Most Affluent
People Make—and Enjoy—Their Riches?" *Forbes*, October 11, 2010, 17.

2. Larry Bartels, *Unequal Democracy: The Political Economy of the New
Gilded Age* (Princeton, NJ: Princeton University Press, 2008).

3. Center for Responsive Politics, "Donor Demographics, 2010," www
.opensecrets.org/bigpicture/donordemographics.php?cycle=2010 (accessed
January 3, 2012).

4. Benjamin Page, Fay Lomax Cook, and Rachel Moskowitz, "Wealthy
Americans, Philanthropy and the Common Good," Institute for Policy
Research, Northwestern University, November 2011. http://www.ipr
.northwestern.edu/publications/workingpapers/wpabstracts11/wp1113.htm
(accessed January 16, 2012). See Jordan Howard, "Wealthy More Likely to
Contact Congress, Study Says," *Huffington Post*, November 8, 2011, www
.huffingtonpost.com/2011/11/08/wealthy-congress-contact-study_n_1081740
.html (accessed January 3, 2012).

5. Ibid., "Wealthy Americans."

6. Foundation Center Statistical Information Center, "National Growth
Data," http://foundationcenter.org/findfunders/statistics/pdf/02_found
_growth/2009/03_09.pdf (accessed January 3, 2012).

7. See Peter Dreier and Chuck Collins, "Traitors to Their Class: Social
Change Philanthropy and Movements for Change," *New Labor Forum*,
Winter 2012.

8. Jeff Zeleny and Megah Thee-Brenan, "New Poll Finds a Deep Distrust
of Government," *New York Times*, October 25, 2011, www.nytimes.com
/2011/10/26/us/politics/poll-finds-anxiety-on-the-economy-fuels-volatility-in
-the-2012-race.html. (accessed January 3, 2012).

9. Page, Cook, and Moskowitz, "Wealthy Americans."

10. Ed Pilkington, "Koch Brothers: Secretive Billionaires to Launch Vast
Database with 2012 in Mind," *Guardian*, November 7, 2011, www.guardian
.co.uk/world/2011/nov/07/koch-brothers-database-2012-election (accessed
January 3, 2012).

11. Charitable donors in the top 1 percent are in the top tax bracket of
35 percent and are able to substantially reduce their taxes with charitable
deductions. See William Randolph, "Charitable Deductions, Department of

Treasury," Tax Policy Center, www.taxpolicycenter.org/taxtopics/encyclopedia
/Charitable-Deductions.cfm (accessed January 3, 2012).

12. Robert Lenzner, "The Top 0.1% of the Nation Earn Half of All
Capital Gains," *Forbes*, November 21, 2011, http://news.yahoo.com/top-0-1
-nation-earn-half-capital-gains-172647859.html (accessed January 3, 2012).

13. Stefan Karlsson, "Income Inequality: What's the Impact of Free Trade
and Immigration?" *Christian Science Monitor*, October 27, 2010, www
.csmonitor.com/Business/Stefan-Karlsson/2010/1027/Income-inequality
-What-s-the-impact-of-free-trade-and-immigration (accessed January 3,
2012).

Chapter 4: Life in the 99 Percent

1. "Trends in the Distribution of Household Income Between 1979 and
2007," Congressional Budget Office, October 2011, www.cbo.gov/doc.cfm
?index=12485Name (accessed January 3, 2012). Also see "America's Tilt to
the Top: The Deepest Stats Yet," Inequality.org, http://inequality.org/tilt-top
-deepest-stats (accessed January 3, 2012).

2. Sylvia A. Allegretto, "The State of Working America's Wealth,"
Economic Policy Institute, Briefing Paper #292, March 23, 2011.

3. "Union Members Summary," Bureau of Labor Statistics, U.S.
Department of Labor, January 21, 2011, www.bls.gov/news.release/union2
.nr0.htm (accessed January 3, 2012).

4. Robert Putnam, *Bowling Alone: The Collapse and Revival of American
Community* (New York: Simon and Schuster, 2000).

5. Michael I. Norton and Dan Ariely, "Building a Better America—One
Wealth Quintile at a Time," *Perspectives on Psychological Science* 6, 1 (2011):
9, www.people.hbs.edu/mnorton/norton%20ariely%20in%20press.pdf
(accessed January 3, 2012).

6. John DeGraaf and David Batker, *What Is the Economy For, Anyway:
Why It's Time to Stop Chasing Growth and Start Pursuing Happiness.* (New
York: Bloomsbury, 2011).

7. Also see Allegretto, "The State of Working America's Wealth," 10–14.

8. Paul Taylor, Richard Fry, and Rakesh Kochhar, "Wealth Gaps Rise to
Record Highs Between Whites, Blacks, Hispanics," Pew Research Center,
July 26, 2011, www.pewsocialtrends.org/2011/07/26/wealth-gaps-rise-to
-record-highs-between-whites-blacks-hispanics (accessed January 3, 2012).

9. Ira Katznelson, *When Affirmative Action Was White: An Untold History
of Racial Inequality in Twentieth-Century America* (New York: W. W. Norton,
2005).

Chapter 5: The Wall Street Inequality Machine

1. Testimony of Simon Johnson, Congressional Oversight Panel, *An Overall Assessment of TARP and Financial Stability*, 112th Congress, 1st session, 2011, 118–123, http://frwebgate.access.gpo.gov/cgi-bin/getdoc.cgi ?dbname=112_senate_hearings&docid=f:65276.wais (accessed January 3, 2012).

2. Center for Responsive Politics, "Donor Demographics, 2010," www .opensecrets.org/bigpicture/donordemographics.php?cycle=2010 (accessed January 3, 2012).

3. Louise Story, "Executive Pay," *New York Times*, December 5, 2011, http://topics.nytimes.com/top/reference/timestopics/subjects/e/executive _pay/index.html (accessed January 3, 2012). Estimates that the financial sector now accounts for about 30 percent of the economy's operating profits: Annie Lowrey, "More Profits, Fewer Jobs," Slate.com, March 28, 2011, www .slate.com/articles/business/moneybox/2011/03/more_profits_fewer_jobs. html (accessed January 3, 2012). Also see Bureau of Economic Analysis, "National Income and Product Accounts," December 22, 2011, www.bea.gov/newsreleases/national/gdp/gdpnewsrelease.htm (accessed January 3, 2012).

4. Lawrence Mishel and Josh Bivens, "Occupy Wall Streeters Are Right About Skewed Economic Rewards in the United States," Economic Policy Institute, Briefing Paper #331, October 26, 2011, www.epi.org/files/2011 /BriefingPaper331.pdf (accessed January 3, 2012).

5. Vincent Trivett, "25 US Mega Corporations: Where They Rank if They Were Countries," *Business Insider*, June 27, 2011, www.businessinsider .com/25-corporations-bigger-than-countries-2011-6?op=1 (accessed January 3, 2012).

6. For over eighteen years, I've coauthored reports on "Executive Excess" examining different aspects of CEO compensation issues. See www.ips-dc .org/executiveexcess.

7. Sarah Anderson, Chuck Collins, Scott Klinger, and Sam Pizzi-gati, "The Massive CEO Rewards for Tax Dodging," Institute for Policy Studies, August 31, 2011, www.ips-dc.org/reports/executive_excess _2011_the_massive_ceo_rewards_for_tax_dodging (accessed January 3, 2012).

8. David Olive, "Business Guru Roger Martin Calls for CEO Pay Reform," *Star*, May 3, 2011, www.thestar.com/business/markets/article /985164—olive-business-guru-rogermartin-calls-for-ceo-pay-reform (accessed January 3, 2012).

9. Anderson et al., "Massive CEO Rewards."

10. Bob Ivry and Christopher Donville, "Black Liquor Tax Boondoggle May Net Billions for Papermakers," Bloomberg, April 17, 2009, www .bloomberg.com/apps/news?pid=newsarchive&sid=abDjfGgdumh4

11. International Paper Company, 10-K report for fiscal year 2010, www .sec.gov/Archives/edgar/data/51434/000119312511046928/d10k.htm (accessed January 3, 2012).

12. David Kocieniewski, "G.E.'s Strategies Let It Avoid Taxes Altogether," *New York Times*, March 24, 2011, www.nytimes.com/2011/03/25/business /economy/25tax.html?pagewanted=all (accessed January 3, 2012).

13. Small Business Administration, *The Small Business Economy: A Report to the President* (Washington, DC: GPO, 2010), 26–27, www.sba.gov/sites /default/files/sb_econ2010.pdf (accessed January 3. 2012).

14. Dane Stangler and Robert E. Litan, "Where Will the Jobs Come From?" Ewing Marion Kauffman Foundation, 2009.

15. U.S. Census Bureau, "Number of Establishments with Corresponding Employment Change by Employment Size of the Enterprise for the United States and All States, Totals: 2008-2009," www2.census.gov/econ/susb/data /dynamic/0809/us_state_totals_emplchange_2008-2009.xls (accessed January 3, 2012).

16. New research is looking at scale and location of ownership of businesses and how that shapes their environmental perspective. An Environmental Protection Agency (EPA) study found that the average amount of toxins released by absentee-owned facilities or those with out-of-state headquarters is nearly three times more than that of plants with in-state headquarters, and fifteen times more than that of single-location enterprises. Don Grant et al., "Are Subsidiaries More Prone to Pollute?" *Social Science Quarterly* 84, 1 (March 2003): 162–73. See also National Center for Environmental Economics, U.S. Environmental Protection Agency, "Organizational Structures, Citizen Participation, and Corporate Environmental Performance," http://yosemite .epa.gov/ee/epa/eed.nsf/08fff10959725aba852575a6006ab35f/264b4f97e5fae 287852575a7005e9396%21OpenDocument (accessed January 3, 2012).

17. Citizens for Tax Justice, "Corporate Taxpayers and Corporate Tax Dodgers, 2008–2010," November 2011, http://ctj.org/corporatetaxdodgers (accessed January 3, 2012).

Chapter 6: How Inequality Wrecks Everything We Care About

1. According to the Center for Responsive Politics, there were 12,220 registered lobbyists in 2011. This is 22.84 lobbyists for every one of the 535

members of Congress. Center for Responsive Politics, "Lobbying Database," www.opensecrets.org/lobby/index.php?ql3 (accessed January 3, 2012).

2. For a good overview of health and inequality issues, see Sam Pizzigati, *Greed and Good: Understanding and Overcoming the Inequality That Limits Our Lives* (New York: Apex Press, 2004), 311–30. Also see Dr. Stephen Bezruchka's website, Population Health Forum (http://depts.washington.edu /eqhlth), for information on global and U.S. health and inequality information. Also see Stephen Bezruchka and M. A. Mercer, "The Lethal Divide: How Economic Inequality Affects Health," in M. Fort, M. A. Mercer, and O. Gish, eds., *Sickness and Wealth: The Corporate Assault on Global Health* (Boston: South End Press, 2004), 11–18.

3. See Richard Wilkinson, *Unhealthy Societies: The Afflictions of Inequality* (London: Routledge, 1996).

4. Sean F. Reardon and Kendra Bischoff, "Growth in the Residential Segregation of Families by Income, 1970–2009," Stanford University, US 2010 Project, Russell Sage Foundation, and American Communities Project at Brown University, November 2011, www.s4.brown.edu/us2010/Data /Report/report111111.pdf (accessed January 3, 2012).

5. Edward J. Blakely and Mary Gail Snyder, *Fortress America: Gated Communities in the United States* (Washington, DC: Brookings Institution Press, 1997); and Justice Policy Institute study, as reported in Jesse Katy, "A Nation of Too Many Prisoners?" *Los Angeles Times*, February 15, 2000.

6. Wojciech Kopczuk, Emmanuel Saez, and Jae Song, "Earnings Inequality and Mobility in the United States: Evidence from Social Security Data Since 1937," *Quarterly Journal of Economics* 125, 1 (February 2010): 91–128, http://ideas.repec.org/a/tpr/qjecon/v125y2010i1p91-128.html (accessed January 3, 2012).

7. OECD, "A Family Affair: Intergenerational Social Mobility Across OECD Countries," *Economic Policy Reforms: Going for Growth*, www.oecd .org/dataoecd/2/7/45002641.pdf (accessed January 3, 2012). Also see the Pew Charitable Trust's Economic Mobility Project (www.economicmobility.org) and their study "Chasing the Same Dream, Climbing Different Ladders: Economic Mobility in the United States and Canada," January 2010, www .economicmobility.org/reports_and_research/other/other?id=0012 (accessed January 3, 2012).

8. Bill Gates Sr. and Chuck Collins, *Wealth and Our Commonwealth: Why American Should Tax Accumulated Fortunes* (Boston: Beacon Press, 2003).

9. Ibid., 19–22.

10. David Lynch, "How Inequality Hurts the Economy," *Business Week Insider*, November 16, 2011, www.businessweek.com/magazine/how

-inequality-hurts-the-economy-11162011.html?campaign_id=rss_topStories
(accessed January 3, 2012).

11. Ibid.

12. Raghuram G. Rajan, *Fault Lines: How Hidden Fractures Still Threaten the World Economy* (Princeton, NJ: Princeton Unversity Press, 2010).

Chapter 7: How Wealth Inequality Crashed the Economy

1. One recommended book on the economic meltdown is Ron Suskind, *Confidence Men: Wall Street, Washington, and the Education of a President* (New York: HarperCollins, 2011).

2. James Lardner et al., *Up to Our Eyeballs: The Hidden Truths and Consequences of Debt in Today's America* (New York: New Press, 2008).

3. See Matt Taibbi, "Wikileaks: Speculators Helped Cause Oil Bubble," *Rolling Stone*, May 26, 2011, www.rollingstone.com/politics/blogs/taibblog /wikileaks-cables-show-speculators-behind-oil-bubble-20110526 (accessed January 3, 2012).

4. Ibid. Senator Dick Durbin (D-Ill.) pressed for hearings and legislation to respond to oil speculation in 2008; see Mose Buchele, "Durbin Urges Probe of Gas Prices," Progress Illinois, April 24, 2008, www.progressillinois.com/2008 /04/24/durbin-urges-probe-of-gas-prices (accessed January 3, 2012).

Chapter 8: The Sleeping 99 Percent Giant Wakes Up

1. Merrill Lynch Global Wealth Management and Capgemini, "15th Annual World Wealth Report," June 22, 2011, www.capgemini.com/news -and-events/news/merrill-lynch-global-wealth-management-and-capgemini -release-15th-annual-world-wealth-report (accessed January 3, 2012).

2. See the US Uncut website, www.usuncut.org.

3. Nicholas Kulish, "As Scorn for Vote Grows, Protests Surge Around Globe," *New York Times*, September 28, 2011, A1.

4. See the Rebuild the Dream website at www.rebuildthedream.com.

5. See the Move Your Money website at http://moveyourmoneyproject .org and the New Bottom Line campaign at www.newbottomline.com/move _our_money.

6. See National Nurses United at www.nationalnursesunited.org.

7. See "Circle of Protection: A Statement on Why We Need to Protect Programs for the Poor," Sojourners, https://secure3.convio.net/sojo/site

/Advocacy?cmd=display&page=UserAction&id=419 (accessed January 3, 2012).

8. See the Caring Across Generations website at http://caringacrossgenera tions.org.

9. Groups leading the effort to pass legislation opposing tax havens include US Uncut (www.usuncut.org) and the Financial Accountability and Corporate Transparency (FACT) coalition (http://fact.gfintegrity.org).

10. See also Institute for Policy Studies, "America Is Not Broke," November 21, 2011, www.ips-dc.org/reports/america_is_not_broke (accessed January 3, 2012).

11. Elspeth Gilmore is the co-director of Resource Generation. See her statement at http://westandwiththe99percent.tumblr.com/post/11338251599 (accessed January 3, 2012).

12. See Brian Miller and Mike Lapham, *The Self-Made Myth: And the Truth About How Government Helps Individuals and Businesses Succeed* (San Francisco, CA: Berrett Koehler, 2012).

Chapter 9: Reversing the Inequality Death Spiral

1. There are a number of organizations and networks emerging to develop a framework for this transition to a new economy and support transition institutions. These include the New Economy Working Group (www.neweconomyworkinggroup.org), the New Economy Network (www.neweconomynetwork.org), the New Economics Institute (www.neweconomicsinstitute.org), and the Post Carbon Institute (www .postcarbon.org).

2. See Lawrence Goodwyn, *The Populist Moment: A Short History of the Agrarian Revolt in America* (New York: Oxford University Press, 1978); and Sam Pizzigati, *Greed and Good: Understanding and Overcoming the Inequality That Limits Our Lives* (New York: Apex Press, 2004).

Chapter 10: Bold Rule Changes to Break Up Concentrated Wealth

1. David Lynch, "How Inequality Hurts the Economy," *Business Week Insider*, November 16, 2011, www.businessweek.com/magazine/how -inequality-hurts-the-economy-11162011.html?campaign_id=rss_topStories (accessed January 3, 2012).

2. See Bill Gates Sr. and Chuck Collins, *Wealth and Our Commonwealth: Why American Should Tax Accumulated Fortunes* (Boston: Beacon Press, 2003).

3. Alison Goldberg, Chuck Collins, Sam Pizzigati, and Scott Klinger, "Unnecessary Austerity: U.S. Deficits Worsened by Failure to Tax Millionaires and Tax Dodging Corporations," Institute for Policy Studies, Program on Inequality and the Common Good, April 2011, www.ips-dc.org/reports /unnecessary_austerity_unnecessary_government_shutdown (accessed February 6, 2012).

4. Ibid.

5. Amy Bingham, "Almost 1,500 Millionaires Do Not Pay Income Tax," ABC News, August 6, 2011, http://abcnews.go.com/Politics/1500 -millionaires-pay-income-tax/story?id=14242254#.TrwQYWDdLwN (accessed January 3, 2012).

6. Sam Pizzigati, "The New Forbes 400—and Their $1.5 Trillion," Inequality.org, September 25, 2011, http://inequality.org/forbes-400-15 -trillion (accessed January 3, 2012).

7. Adam Davidson, "It's Not Just About the Millionaires," *New York Times*, November 9, 2011, www.nytimes.com/2011/11/13/magazine/adam -davidson-tax-middle-class.html (accessed January 3, 2012).

8. See David Callahan, *Kindred Spirits: Harvard Business School's Extraordinary Class of 1949 and How They Transformed American Business* (Hoboken, NJ: Wiley, 2002).

9. Rick Wartzman, "Put a Cap on CEO Pay," *Business Week*, September 12, 2008, www.businessweek.com/managing/content/sep2008/ca20080912 _186533.htm (accessed January 3, 2012).

10. For a review of the literature, see "The Ineffective Enterprise," a discussion that appears in Pizzigati, *Greed and Good.*

11. Sam Pizzigati, "The Paycheck Data CEOs Don't Want Us to See," *Too Much*, January 8, 2011, http://toomuchonline.org/the-paycheck-data-ceos -dont-want-us-to-see (accessed January 3, 2012).

12. Sarah Anderson, John Cavanagh, Chuck Collins, Mike Lapham, and Sam Pizzigati, "Executive Excess 2008: How Average Taxpayers Subsidize Runaway Pay," Institute for Policy Studies, August 25, 2008, www.ips-dc .org/reports/executive_excess_2008_how_average_taxpayers_subsidize _runaway_pay (accessed January 3, 2012).

13. Lucian A. Bebchuk and Yaniv Grinstein, "The Growth of Executive Pay," *Oxford Review of Economic Policy*, Summer 2005.

14. Introduced by Rep. Jan Schakowsky (D-Ill.), the Patriot Corporations Act (HR 1163 in the 112th Congress). See: www.opencongress.org/bill/112 -h1163/show; and a background article by Sam Pizzigati, "Can We Cut CEO

Pay Down to Size?" *Yes,* September 1, 2010, www.yesmagazine.org/new-economy/can-we-cut-ceo-pay-down-to-size.

15. Frank Knapp, "Statement at Press Conference," Business and Investors Against Tax Haven Abuse, October 11, 2011, http://businessagainsttaxhavens.org/press-release-small-businesses-agree-with-new-senate-study-don%E2%80%99t-reward-job-destroyers-with-another-tax-holiday (accessed January 3, 2012).

16. Nicholas Shaxson, *Treasure Islands: Uncovering the Damage of Offshore Banking and Tax Havens* (Basingstroke, Hampshire: Palgrave Macmillan, 2011).

17. David Kocieniewski, "G.E.'s Strategies Let It Avoid Taxes Altogether," *New York Times,* March 24, 2010, www.nytimes.com/2011/03/25/business/economy/25tax.html?_r=2 (accessed January 3, 2012).

18. The Stop Tax Haven Abuse Act was introduced in the 112th Congress by Senator Carl Levin (D-Mich.) in the Senate as S 2669, and by Representative Lloyd Doggett (D-Tex.) in the House, as HR 2669. For a summary of the legislation, see Senator Carl Levin's website, "Summary of the Stop Tax Haven Abuse Act of 2011," July 12, 2011, http://levin.senate.gov/newsroom/press/release/summary-of-the-stop-tax-haven-abuse-act-of-2011/?section=alltypes.

19. David Korten, "How to Liberate America from Wall Street Rule," New Economy Working Group, July 2011, 6, http://neweconomyworkinggroup.org/report/how-liberate-america-wall-street-rule.

20. See www.moveourmoneyusa.org, http://moveyourmoneyproject.org, and the New Bottom Line Campaign to move $1 billion, www.newbottomline.com/new_bottom_line_money_movers_pull_nearly_50_million_from_big_banks.

21. Korten, "How to Liberate America."

22. The range of emerging business organizations that support high-road and healthy economic policies includes the American Sustainable Business Council (www.asbcouncil.org), Main Street Alliance (www.mainstreetalliance.org), Business for Shared Prosperity (www.businessforsharedprosperity.org), and Small Business Majority (www.smallbusinessmajority.org).

23. Strategic Corporate Initiative, "Toward a Global Citizens Movement to Bring Corporations Back Under Control," Corporate Ethics International, 2007, http://corpethics.org/section.php?id=17 (accessed January 3, 2012).

24. For inspiring examples about the impact of shareholder activism, see the website of the Interfaith Center on Corporate Responsibility, www.iccr.org.

25. Forum for Sustainable and Responsible Investment, "2010 Report on Socially Responsible Investing Trends in the United States," 2010,

http://ussif.org/resources/research/documents/2010TrendsES.pdf (accessed January 3, 2012).

26. Someone like Warren Buffett gets preferential tax treatment and is taxed at only 15 percent. Meanwhile, the earned wages of a doctor, teacher, or a scientist in a top income tax bracket will be taxed at a 35 percent rate.

27. Figures represent an annualized average of cuts recommended over a five-year time period in Andrew Fieldhouse, "The People's Budget: A Technical Analysis," Economic Policy Institute, http://grijalva.house.gov /uploads/The%20People%27s%20Budget%20-%20A%20Technical %20Analysis.pdf.

28. Dean Baker, "The Deficit-Reducing Potential of a Financial Specula-tion Tax," Center for Economic and Policy Research, January 2011, www .cepr.net/documents/publications/fst-2011-01.pdf (accessed January 3, 2012). Note: In November 2011, Rep. Peter DeFazio (D.-Ore.) and Senator Tom Harkin (D-Iowa) introduced bills to create a U.S. financial transaction tax at a lower tax rate than that calculated by CEPR. At a rate of 0.03 percent on each transaction, the Joint Committee on Taxation estimated that these bills would generate $353 billion in revenues over ten years.

29. Sarah Anderson et al., "High Flyers: How Private Jet Travel Is Straining the System, Warming the Planet, and Costing You Money," Institute for Policy Studies, June 2008, www.ips-dc.org/reports/high_flyers (accessed January 3, 2012).

30. Gilbert E. Metcalf and David Weisbach, "The Design of a Carbon Tax," *Harvard Environmental Law Review*, January 2009, www.law.harvard .edu/students/orgs/elr/vol33_2/Metcalf%20 Weisbach.pdf (accessed January 3, 2012).

Conclusion

1. "Full Text of Barack Obama's Speech in Osawtomie, Kansas," *Guardian*, Tuesday, December 6, 2011, www.guardian.co.uk/world/2011 /dec/07/full-text-barack-obama-speech.

Resources

For a complete list of books, see the Resources section at http://
inequality.org. For activist organizations, visit http://inequality.org
/organizations.

Acknowledgments

It takes a village to write a book, even a short book.

A special thanks to the good people at Berrett-Koehler Publishers, who approached me about writing to respond to this historical moment. It was a wonderful invitation, and what you hold in your hands is the result of this collaboration.

Thanks to the people who read this manuscript in various forms and offered detailed comments. Special thanks to Sam Pizzigati and Andrea Gordillo, who helped with reviewing and researching. Thanks to readers Josh O'Conner, Robert Ellman, Jeff Kulick, David Korten, Daniel Moss, Mary Hannon, Sarah Anderson, John Cavanagh, Salvatore Babones, and Alison Goldberg.

Thanks to several of my colleagues at the Institute for Policy Studies who have been great allies in this process, including Scott Klinger, Bob Keener, Sarah Byrnes, Liz Wambui, Gillian Mason, and Heather Carito. Thanks to the members of the New Economy Working Group and several colleagues who added encouragement along the way, including Barbara Ehrenreich, Peter Barnes, Adam Hochschild, Helen Cohen, Mark Lipman, and Mike Miller.

Thanks to those who provided encouragement and hospitality along the way, including Dakota Butterfield, Chris Cartter, Mikal

Gaines, Nora Collins, Tricia Brennan, Barbara and Ed Collins, and Vilunya Diskin. A special thanks to Mary, who created a sense of home while I worked on this book and helped midwife this book with listening, food, humor, grace, and a ton of useful suggestions, especially with the conclusion.

Index

About the Author

Photo © Lori DeSantis.

Chuck Collins is a senior scholar at the Institute for Policy Studies (IPS) and directs IPS's Program on Inequality and the Common Good. He co-edits the Web resource www.inequality.org, which offers data, analysis, and commentary.

He is co-founder of Wealth for the Common Good (www.wealthforcommongood.org), a national network of business leaders, small business owners, and wealthy individuals concerned about tax fairness and shared prosperity.

He is co-author, with Bill Gates Sr., of *Wealth and Our Commonwealth* (Beacon Press, 2003), a case for taxing inherited wealth and preserving the federal estate tax.

He is an expert on U.S. inequality and the economic crisis. In 1995, he co-founded United for a Fair Economy with S. M. Miller and the late Felice Yeskel to educate the public about inequality issues. He co-authored, with Felice Yeskel, *Economic Apartheid in America: A Primer on Economic Inequality and Insecurity* (New Press, 2005).

With Mary Wright, he is co-author of *The Moral Measure of the Economy* (Orbis, 2005), which examines Christian perspectives on U.S. economic life. It was named as one of the Best Spiritual Books of 2007, according to *Spirituality and Practice*. He also co-authored, with Nick Thorkelson, a comic book on the economic crisis, *The Economic Meltdown Funnies*.

He lives in Boston, Massachusetts.

Berrett–Koehler
Publishers

Berrett-Koehler is an independent publisher dedicated to an ambitious mission: *Creating a World That Works for All*.

We believe that to truly create a better world, action is needed at all levels—individual, organizational, and societal. At the individual level, our publications help people align their lives with their values and with their aspirations for a better world. At the organizational level, our publications promote progressive leadership and management practices, socially responsible approaches to business, and humane and effective organizations. At the societal level, our publications advance social and economic justice, shared prosperity, sustainability, and new solutions to national and global issues.

A major theme of our publications is "Opening Up New Space." Berrett-Koehler titles challenge conventional thinking, introduce new ideas, and foster positive change. Their common quest is changing the underlying beliefs, mindsets, institutions, and structures that keep generating the same cycles of problems, no matter who our leaders are or what improvement programs we adopt.

We strive to practice what we preach—to operate our publishing company in line with the ideas in our books. At the core of our approach is stewardship, which we define as a deep sense of responsibility to administer the company for the benefit of all of our "stakeholder" groups: authors, customers, employees, investors, service providers, and the communities and environment around us.

We are grateful to the thousands of readers, authors, and other friends of the company who consider themselves to be part of the "BK Community." We hope that you, too, will join us in our mission.

A BK Currents Book

This book is part of our BK Currents series. BK Currents books advance social and economic justice by exploring the critical intersections between business and society. Offering a unique combination of thoughtful analysis and progressive alternatives, BK Currents books promote positive change at the national and global levels. To find out more, visit **www.bkconnection.com**.

Berrett–Koehler
Publishers

A community dedicated to creating
a world that works for all

Visit Our Website: www.bkconnection.com

Read book excerpts, see author videos and Internet movies, read
our authors' blogs, join discussion groups, download book apps, find
out about the BK Affiliate Network, browse subject-area libraries of
books, get special discounts, and more!

Subscribe to Our Free E-Newsletter, the *BK Communiqué*

Be the first to hear about new publications, special discount offers,
exclusive articles, news about bestsellers, and more! Get on the list
for our free e-newsletter by going to **www.bkconnection.com**.

Get Quantity Discounts

Berrett-Koehler books are available at quantity discounts for orders
of ten or more copies. Please call us toll-free at (800) 929-2929 or
email us at **bkp.orders@aidcvt.com**.

Join the BK Community

BKcommunity.com is a virtual meeting place where people from
around the world can engage with kindred spirits to create a world
that works for all. BKcommunity.com members may create their own
profiles, blog, start and participate in forums and discussion groups,
post photos and videos, answer surveys, announce and register for
upcoming events, and chat with others online in real time. Please join
the conversation!

Certified
Corporation
bcorporation.net